On 15 April 1989, Terry Fitzgibbon and his two sons survived the Hillsborough disaster. Nine years later his struggle to come to terms with the tragedy that shook a city is tearing him and his family apart. Haunted by survivor's guilt, Terry is oblivious to the conflict in his own home, the pain he is inflicting on his wife and the very real tragedy that is unfolding for his neighbours.

Jonathan Harvey comes from Liverpool and now lives in London. His plays include: *Cherry Blossom Tree* (Liverpool Playhouse Studio, 1987) which won him the 1987 National Girobank Young Writer of the Year Award; *Mohair* (Royal Court Young Writers Festival, London/International Festival of Young Playwrights, Sydney, 1988); *Tripping and Falling* (Glasshouse Theatre Company, Manchester, 1989); *Catch* (Spring Street Theatre, Hull, 1990); *Lady Snogs The Blues* (Lincoln Arts Festival, 1991); *Wildfire* (Royal Court Theatre Upstairs, 1992); *Beautiful Thing* (Bush Theatre, London, 1993 and Donmar Warehouse, London/Duke of York's Theatre, London, 1994) winner of the John Whiting Award 1994; *Babies* (Royal National Theatre Studio/Royal Court Theatre, 1994), winner of the George Devine Award 1993 and *Evening Standard*'s Most Promising Playwright Award 1994; *Boom Bang-A-Bang* (Bush Theatre, 1995); *Rupert Street Lonely Hearts Club* (English Touring Theatre/Contact Theatre Company, 1995) winner, *Manchester Evening News* Best New Play Award, 1996; *Swan Song* (Pleasance, Edinburgh/Hampstead Theatre, London, 1997). Television and film work includes: *West End Girls* (Carlton); *Beautiful Thing* (Channel Four/Island World Productions), *Gimme, Gimme, Gimme* (Tiger Aspect/BBC2), *Dinner At Tiffany's*, an episode of *Murder Most Horrid* (BBC2).

by the same author

plays
Beautiful Thing
Babies
Boom Bang-A-Bang
Rupert Street Lonely Hearts Club

screenplay
Beautiful Thing

GUIDING STAR

Jonathan Harvey

Methuen

Copyright © 1998 by Jonathan Harvey
The right of Jonathan Harvey to be identified as the author of this work
has been asserted by him in accordance with the Copyright, Designs and
Patents Act, 1988

First published in Great Britain in 1998
by Methuen Publishing Limited
20 Vauxhall Bridge Road, London, SW1V 2SA

Random House Australia (Pty) Limited
20 Alfred Street, Milsons Point, Sydney, New South Wales 2061, Australia

Random House New Zealand Limited
18 Poland Road, Glenfield, Auckland 10, New Zealand

Random House South Africa (Pty) Limited
Endulini, 5a Jubilee Road, Parktown 2193, South Africa

Methuen Publishing Limited Reg. No. 3543167

A CIP catalogue record for this book is available from the British Library

ISBN 0 413 73610 5

Typeset by SX Composing DTP, Rayleigh, Essex
Printed and bound in Great Britain
by Cox & Wyman Ltd, Reading, Berkshire

Guiding Star

Guiding Star was first performed at the Everyman Theatre, Liverpool, on 25 September 1998 and subsequently transferred to the Cottesloe auditorium at the Royal National Theatre, London, on 5 November 1998. The cast was as follows:

Terry	Colin Tierney
Carol	Tracey Wilkinson
Marni	Tina Malone
Laurence	Kieran O'Brien
Liam	Carl Rice
Gina	Samantha Lavelle
Charlie	Jake Abraham
Man in Woods	Robert Perkins
Joanne	Elaine Lordan

Directed by Gemma Bodinetz
Designed by Bruce Macadie
Lighting by Tina MacHugh
Music by Richard Harvey

Characters

Terry Fitzgibbon, *thirty-three, world-weary Liverpudlian. A good-looking fella who's let himself go in the last few years. An unassuming man who is always apologising for himself.*
Carol Fitzgibbon, *thirty-three, Terry's patient wife. Attractive and slightly built.*
Laurence Fitzgibbon, *seventeen, Terry and Carol's eldest son. A bit of a scally.*
Liam Fitzgibbon, *fifteen, Laurence's younger brother. Quiet and a bit spotty.*
Marni Sweet, *thirty-five, Carol's best friend and neighbour. A bit overweight.*
Gina, *nineteen. Pretty and loud. Laurence's girlfriend.*
Charlie Sweet, *thirty-five, Marni's husband and Terry's best mate.*
Joanne, *thirty, a beautiful prostitute from London.*
Man in Woods, *thirty-five, Welsh.*

Setting

The play is set in Liverpool, Tenby and London, 1998.

Act One

Scene One

The Fitzgibbons' back garden.

*The back garden of the Fitzgibbons' council house in the south end of Liverpool. It's quite late at night. It's dark. The back door to the kitchen is open and light creeps out from inside. Two white plastic patio chairs sit near the back door. At the far end of the garden is a rubbish bin. To the right of the Fitzgibbons' garden we can see the start of their neighbours **Charlie** and **Marni**'s garden, and a second rubbish bin. As the scene starts, **Terry Fitzgibbon** is squatting in the soil of the garden, drawing a circle in the soil around him. He turns full circle to do this. He stands up and looks up at the sky, brushing the soil away on his trousers. He is lost in thought. Eventually he walks over to one of the chairs and sits down, staring at his hands. Off, we hear their front door go and eventually **Terry**'s wife **Carol** calling for him.*

Carol (*off*) Terry?! Terry?!

Terry Out here.

*Carol comes to the back door in an overcoat, carrying the remnants of a chip-shop meal. She kisses **Terry** on the forehead.*

Carol Hiya, love. Had a good night?

Terry Yeah.

Carol The kids in bed?

Terry Er, yeah.

She walks down the garden to put her chip paper in the bin.

Carol You'll never guess what happened at bingo.

Terry What?

Carol   Marni won fifty pound. So it was sausage dinners all round on the way home. It's brilliant. She'll be able to get a taxi up the hospital tomorrow, she's made up.

Terry   I bet she is.

Carol   Terry, what's this?

Terry   What?

Carol   Did you do this?

Terry   I seen it on the telly. If you stand in the earth, and you draw a circle in the soil round yourself, it protects you.

Carol   What from?

Terry   I dunno. Bad luck.

Carol   You're going doolally you are.

Terry   I think it's Celtic.

Carol   I don't care what it is, it looks a right mess. What d'you need protecting from?

Terry   I just thought I'd give it a go.

Carol   Have you started talking to the plants as well? I thought I was married to a nice riveter from Ford's. When all along I was married to Prince fucking Charles.

She looks up at the house.

Ay, Terry. I thought you said the kids were in bed.

Terry   What?

Carol   Have they taken to sleeping with the curtains wide open?

Terry   I dunno.

Carol   You'd test the patience of a saint.

Terry   Eh?

She goes inside. **Terry** *sits there. Just then* **Marni** *appears in her garden with some rubbish. She takes it to her bin.*

Marni   Are men congenitally lazy?

Terry   Oright, Marni.

Marni   I ask him to do one little thing while I'm out and he can't even be arsed. One bag of rubbish, to go in the bin. Oh no, too much like hard work.

Terry   I hear you had a win at the bingo.

Marni   Yeah I did. And what does he want? Half of it. I said, 'You can get to fuck.' I'm using that money to get a taxi up the hospital for a week. I'm sick to death of buses. I have three of them to get up to Alder Hey and it does my fucking head in. I don't know if I've got one of those faces that people feel they can just gab at, but honest to God, it's just talk talk talk all the fucking time. This woman today, she gets on the 78, and she takes one look at me and goes, 'What colour's your coat?' I said, 'What are yeh? Blind?' She goes, 'Would you say it was mushroom or brown?' I felt like saying, 'Who gives a shit?' So I just said, 'Beige.' That shut her up. I tell you, there'll be none o'that in a taxi. Though knowing my luck I'll get a driver with verbal diarrhoea.

Carol *rushes back in.*

Carol   This family's going mad. D'you know that?

Marni   Goway?

Marni *gets a ciggie out and lights up.*

Carol   The kids aren't in! Where are they?

Marni   Well, I dunno, I've been out with you.

Carol   Terry?

Terry   I've been sat out here, haven't I? I can't see the front door.

Carol   Honest to God. I turn me back for five minutes to go the bingo and the kids have done a runner. Our Laurence, fine. But our Liam?

Terry   Someone rang.

Carol   He's got school in the morning.

Terry   Who rang?

Carol   It's twenty-five to twelve.

Terry   Someone rang for Liam and he went out. I didn't notice the time go by. Don't panic, Carol.

Carol   Terry. Our fifteen-year-old son who never goes out has done precisely that. The only friend he's got round here's Wayne, and he's in the hospital.

Terry   Maybe he went to visit him.

Marni   He's not having visitors tonight.

Terry   I don't know what time he went out.

Carol   What've you been doing all evening?

Terry   Sitting here.

Carol   Ignoring the kids.

Terry   I've been thinking.

Carol   Nice one, Terry. And both your sons have disappeared.

Marni   Carol, calm down. They're probably out together.

Carol   They can't stand each other.

Marni   Doesn't stop me and my Charlie goin' the pub together.

Terry   It's not funny, Marni. Oh, fuckin'ell, where are they?

Carol   Kids take the piss, Terry. And if you don't say be in by a certain time . . .

Terry   Jesus, where are they, Carol?

Carol   I'm not so worried about Laurence.

Marni   I've got no yardstick, you see.

Terry   Bloody hell, what are we gonna do?

Marni   Coz like, I dunno what time you're supposed to expect fifteen-year-olds back in. I mean, it's a bit different with our Wayne. D'you know what I'm saying?

Carol   You'd expect him in by now, wouldn't yeh?

Marni   Maybe.

Terry   Are you saying we're overreacting?

Marni   No. No. It's just. Well, all them kids that hang round the parade, I mean, they're younger than your Liam and they're there 'til all hours.

Carol   Coz their parents are no fucking good.

Terry   They're all on drugs.

Marni   But it's not really your Liam's style, is it?

Terry   I'm sorry, Carol.

Carol   It's them that's taking the piss.

Terry   Won't your Charlie be wondering where you are?

Marni   I've sent him to bed. Ay, we could jump in your car and drive round looking for him.

Carol   Bit tricky.

Marni   Oh yeah.

Terry   He'll be back. He will.

Carol   If you don't wanna drive it any more I don't see why you don't just sell it.

Terry   I'll get back in it one day. I will.

Carol   You keep saying that.

Pause.

Marni   Could he be round at a mate's?

Carol   What mates does he talk about?

Marni   Hasn't he got a mate in Halewood?

Terry   Surinder?

Marni   Phone him.

Carol   We haven't got the number.

Marni   Do the 1471, see who phoned him earlier.

Carol *drags the phone in from the kitchen and dials 1471.*

Terry   I've met Surinder. His parents own the paint shop by the Leather Bottle.

Marni   It's a call box. Should I phone it?

Marni   Mayslie well.

Terry   What do they call that paint shop?

Carol   They'd be in bed be now.

Marni   Rainbow Paints.

Carol   It's just ringing.

Marni   Rainbow Paints is by the Leather Bottle. I swear to God.

Terry   I'll phone 'em. Oh, Jesus. I don't fuckin' believe this!

Carol   Calm down, Terry!

Suddenly the front door goes and **Laurence** *calls through.*

Laurence (*off. American accent*)   Hi, honey, I'm home!

Terry   Thank God for that!

Marni   Oh, he cracks me up.

Terry Laurence?!

Laurence *pops his head round the door.*

Laurence How do?

Carol Where've you been?

Laurence Went for a pint in town.

Carol Is our Liam wit yer?

Laurence No, but he's coming up the street.

Carol Get him out here now!

Marni There's been murders here like you wouldn't believe!

Laurence Jesus. Nice to see you too.

Laurence *goes back in.*

Marni I'll get offski.

Carol Liam! Get out here!

Terry Carol.

Liam *enters.*

Liam What've I done now?

Carol Where the fuckin'ell have you been?

Terry Don't swear at him, Carol!

Marni See yeh.

Marni *exits.*

Liam The Backy.

Carol You what?

Liam The Backy.

Carol You've been the back field at a quarter to twelve at night?

Terry   Who with?

Liam   Judy.

Carol   Judy who?

Liam   Mrs Raymond's dog.

Carol   Mrs Raymond's dog? Why?

Liam   She's had a fall, hasn't she?

Carol   Oh, has she now? And she expects a fifteen-year-old to be walking round the Backy at this time o'night?

Liam   She give us a cup o'tea when I dropped the dog off. Kept me gabbing. Herbal tea it was.

Carol   I don't care if it was fucking lap song soo shong, you shouldn't be walking round there this time o'night.

Liam   I seen Mrs Raymond's daughter wit the funny eye this avvy by the Parade and she said her mum'd fell and broke her hip. And the dog wasn't getting a walk of a night so I said I didn't mind then Mrs Raymond rang this evening. She rang at half nine.

Carol   Well, how comes when I tried the 1471 it was a payphone?

Liam   Coz she's got one o'them payphones in her house. Them little ones, she has! I told yer exactly where I was goin', Dad.

Carol   But I've just rung that payphone and there was no answer.

Liam   She's dead old, it'd take her ages to get to the phone.

Carol   Oh, I feel ashamed, the poor woman.

Liam   I bet you never had a go at Laurence, did yeh?

Carol   He's earning a wage. If he doesn't get to work on time he gets money docked. You've got school tomorrow.

Liam   It's only a quarter to twelve.

Carol   I don't like you goin' the Backy this time o'night.

Liam   I was helping an old lady out. Would you rather her dog shat and peed all over her house?

Carol   Well, isn't that a lovely turn o'phrase for a fifteen-year-old boy?

Liam   God, you can talk. When you were my age you were pregnant.

Carol   Go to bed.

Liam   At least the strongest thing I've had tonight was a peppermint tea, unlike our Laurence. You have to be eighteen to drink in this country, and how old's he?

Carol   Did you have a coat on?

Liam   Ah, you're doing my head in now.

Liam *exits. Pause.*

Terry   Don't have a go at him. He's got a heart of gold.

Carol   So I was outa me mind wit worry, and all along he'd told you exactly what he was up to. Cheers, love. Nice one. Are you coming up?

Terry   I just wanna have a bit of a think for a while.

Carol   You will come to bed?

Terry   Yeah. Just wanna. You know.

Carol   It's that time of year again. I shoulda realised. Jesus, they could set clocks by you.

Terry   Ah, it's great to have them back safe, isn't it?

Carol   I'm gonna read me book.

Carol *goes indoors.*

Terry   Night, love.

The lights fade.

Scene Two

The Fitzgibbons' front room.

The next day. The room is tidy and clean and reasonably modern. A door leads off to the hall, and a window looks out on to the street.
Terry *sits in an armchair, part of a three-piece suite which isn't that old. He is reading a book about Auschwitz. In front of him a coffee table. He wears the same clothes as he had on last night.* **Carol** *comes in carrying a bin bag of clothes.*

Carol   What's that you're reading?

Terry   It's about Auschwitz. Got it from the library.

Carol   Why?

Terry   I was just thinking about it at work, so popped in there on me way home.

Carol   You're morbid, you are.

Terry   What's in there?

Carol   I'm giving some old clothes to the Community Resource Centre. The kids' mostly. Me and Marni are going down there in a bit.

Terry   Nice one.

Carol   Terry.

Terry   What?

Carol   How are you feeling today?

Terry   Fine, girl. Cushty.

Carol   Ah, I'm made up. You're back from work early.

Terry   Yeah.

Carol Oh, listen, you know your brown suit?

Terry The brown one?

Carol You never wear it no more, do yeh?

Terry It's got flares out here.

Carol Should I stick it in wit this lot?

Terry Ay, I got married in that suit.

Carol I was there.

Terry I could get the legs taken in and the collars altered.

Carol When do you wear a suit?

Terry Funerals. Weddings.

Carol You've got your nice grey Top Man one for all that.

Terry Go'ed then.

Carol No, it's all right.

Terry No, Carol. Chuck it out.

Carol I'm not chucking it out. I'm giving it to the Resource Centre. Some fella'll be glad o'that suit. You'll see him walking round the estate in it.

Terry Someone wit no shame.

Carol Ooh, y'little fashion victim, you!

Carol *chuckles as she goes out.* **Terry** *gets up and looks in the big bag. He roots around. He pulls out a child's Liverpool FC kit top, then shorts. He can't believe they're in there. He sits back with them on his knee, staring at them. The doorbell goes twice in succession.*

Carol (*off*)   Can you get that, Terry?

Terry *doesn't seem to hear. The doorbell goes again. Footsteps off then we hear* **Carol** *letting* **Marni** *in. They say hello then enter, laughing at the seventies brown suit that* **Carol** *is carrying on a hanger.* **Marni***, too, is carrying a bin bag of clothes.*

Carol   Can you believe it?

Marni   Oh, God, Terry, put it on and model it.

Terry   What?

Marni   Oh, come on give us a laugh!

Terry   Carol?

Carol   He walked me down the aisle in this!

Terry   Carol?

Marni   Oh, God, the shame! D'you remember my bridesmaid's dress?

Carol   Ay, I spent a fortune on that!

Marni   Y'what? Three yards o'paisley from Speke Market? You gotta be jokin'!

As they laugh, **Terry** *stands up.*

Terry   Carol, you're not throwing these out.

Pause.

Marni   You'll have a job getting into them, Terry lad.

Pause.

Carol   All right, Terry.

Terry *sits down.*

Terry   How could you, Carol?

Carol   I didn't think.

Pause.

I didn't think, Terry.

Terry   You didn't think?

Carol   No. I didn't. I'm sorry.

Pause. **Marni** *sits down.*

Marni   So what's the gossip? Where was your Liam 'till practically midnight last night?

Terry   There is no gossip.

Marni   Oh, goway? Your son goes missing 'til all hours and there's no gossip? Pull the other one, Terry, it's got big fat bells on it!

Terry   No. There isn't any fucking gossip, all right?

Carol   All right, keep your hair on, Terry. She's only have a laugh.

Terry   He was walking that arl girl's dog.

Marni   Which arl girl?

Terry   The one from the corner.

Carol   Mrs Raymond.

Marni   Jewbags Raymond?

Terry   D'you know she lost a load of her relatives at Auschwitz?

Marni   Old Jewbags?

Terry   And you just sit there on your fat arse dismissing her as old Jewbags?

Marni   Did she, Carol?

Terry   Yes she did. And d'you know how I know? Coz I talk to people about things that matter. Like fucking history. Like fucking losing half your family in a gas chamber. Not like where was our Liam 'til quarter to twelve last night. You can read a book about it if you want! If you can read!

Carol   Terry!

Terry   Just coz you haven't got anything going on in your life, doesn't give you free reign to poke your nose in other people's.

Marni   Well, excuse me, Narky Hole, but I've got plenty going on in my life thank you very much.

Carol   You know that.

Marni   Plenty.

Terry   Sorry, Marni.

Marni   So you fucking should be. And for your information I was in the top group for English at school and you were in the second!

Carol (*to* **Terry**, *about the child's kit*)   I'm not throwing that out, you know.

Terry   Good.

Pause. **Carol** *puts the suit in the bin bag then proceeds to tie it up.*

Marni   I went over the Asda today at Hunts Cross.

Carol   D'you get anything?

Marni   A fake Tommy Hilfiger T-shirt and boxies for our Wayne. It's all he can wear in the hospital, you know.

Carol   Oh, he'll be made up with that.

Marni   You wanna get yourself over there, Carol. They've got some lovely bits.

Carol   Yeah, well, you need a car to get over there, don't you.

Marni   Mm. Shame there's not a driver in the family.

Terry   I've said, haven't I? I'll get back in that car when I'm good and ready.

Carol   I'll get me coat.

Carol *exits.*

Marni   I was made up today. I got in that taxi and the driver never said a word. I said to him halfway up Mackett's Lane, I said, 'What do they call you? Silence of the Lambs?'

He said, 'You're a character.' I said, 'I know, don't tell me.
Cathy from *Wuthering Heights*.' He goes, 'Is that a block of
flats?' I thought, quit while you're ahead, love.

Terry   So the clothes up the Asda are good, are they?

Marni   I didn't know you were that interested in fashion.

Terry   Just being polite.

Marni   God, you don't have to be polite with me.

Terry   Well, shut your big fat winging grid then, I'm sick
o'the sound o'yeh.

Pause.

I'm sorry, Marni.

Marni   What's to do wi'you, eh?

Terry   I shouldn't be havin' a go at you.

Marni   Oh, and who should you be havin' a go at?

Terry   Carol. I just dunno how she could do it.

Marni   Terry, it's in the past.

Terry   Oh, what do you know about anything?

Marni   My Charlie's doesn't half worry about you
sometimes, y'know.

Enter **Carol**, *with coat.*

Carol   Ready?

Terry   There's better things to worry about than me.

Marni   Will you not give counselling another thought? It
worked for him.

Terry   I'm not your Charlie.

Marni   You're missing work. They've been awful good to
yeh. I mean, how many more sickies can you take? Goodwill
doesn't last for ever.

Carol   Have you been taking sickies?

Terry   Well, I won't be taking any more.

Marni   If you want, Terry la'.

Terry   I won't.

Carol   Come on, Marni.

Terry   I won't coz I'm not goin' back.

Carol   See you later.

Terry   I walked out.

Carol and **Marni** *stand in the doorway, gobsmacked.*

Carol   You did what?

Terry   Someone'll be glad o'that job. I used to be. Anyone can do it.

Carol   Tell me you're jokin'.

Terry *shakes his head.*

Carol   Tell me you're jokin'!

Terry   I don't tell jokes. You know that. I haven't cracked a joke since 1989. Haven't cracked a joke, or a smile, or been anything but morbidity itself. If I'm pissing yer off, tough shite. I'm all right. If I'm here in this house I'm all right.

Pause.

Marni   I'll take these.

Terry   You go an'all, Carol.

Marni   No, I can take them.

Terry   Take her with y', Marni.

Carol (*hands **Marni** her bag*)   I'll see you later.

Marni   OK.

Marni *goes. We hear the front door slam.* **Carol** *stands in the doorway.*

Carol   I don't *believe* you.

Terry   Believe it.

Carol   No. I don't believe *you.*

Pause.

What did you do?

Terry   I told yeh.

Carol   You know this is it now, don't yeh?

Terry   If you hurry you'll catch Marni.

Carol (*lights a cigarette*)   I don't wanna catch Marni. I wanna stay here and sort this out.

Terry   There's nothing to sort out. It's done.

Carol   Or maybe I should catch Marni. Get them clothes back. There'll be no new glad rags now. I thought we were gonna rig Liam out for his birthday. Best we get his old pullies and sweaters and tell him to make do.

Terry   I'm sorry.

Carol   No you're not. If you had any feeling left in yeh, y'wouldn't have done this.

Terry   I have got feelings, Carol.

Carol   Have yeh?

Pause.

You can only have a go at me in front of Marni, can't you? You can only answer back then.

Terry   I've got feelings.

Carol   Yeah and it's all locked up in there. With a sign, 'Keep Out'.

Pause.

I try to get to you, Terry. And you've littered yourself with a minefield. I don't know where the bombs are, but when I hit one . . . Christ, do I know it.

Pause.

Why?

Terry   You know why.

Carol   How can I know unless you tell me? You know more about Mrs Raymond from the corner than you do about me. Say you talk about things that matter. You're a liar.

Terry *lowers his head and starts to weep silently.* **Carol** *goes to him and takes the football kit from him.*

Terry   What you doing?

Carol   I'm gonna put it upstairs. In your drawer. The lads don't wannit any more.

Terry   Liam's usually back by now.

Carol   He's gone up the hospital to see Wayne.

Terry   And where's our Laurence?

The front door goes, off.

Carol   That'll be him now.

Laurence *enters.*

Laurence   Oright?

Carol   Never better. (*She exits.*)

Laurence   Has she got a cob-on?

Terry   Time o'the month, lad.

Laurence   Ay, Dad, you couldn't lend us twenty quid, could yeh? I've asked this bird out from work and when I tried to get money out the cashy it said there was nothing left in me account. Oh, go on, Dad. I get paid on Friday, I'll pay you back then.

Terry   Who's this bird?

Laurence   Gina. Ah, Dad, she's dead fit.

Terry   I've never heard you mention her before.

Laurence   She only started today, thought I better get in quick.

Terry   Where yous goin'?

Laurence   Town. Meeting her under Dicky Lewis at half eight.

Terry   I've only got fifteen.

Laurence   Ah, well, give us that then I can ask me mum for a fiver.

Terry   Oh, don't ask your mam, Laurence.

Laurence   She's not gonna deny me five fuckin' quid.

Terry   She's in a funny mood. I'll give Charlie a knock.

Laurence   But me mam won't mind.

Terry   Don't say nothing to her. Charlie's loaded. Marni had a win on the bingo.

Terry *goes out. The door slams off.* **Laurence** *switches the telly on and puts his feet up on the coffee table.* **Carol** *comes in.*

Carol   I thought you'd gone back out. Was it your dad?

Laurence   Dunno. Musta been.

Carol   Where's he goin'? (*She looks out of the window.*) He's knocking for Charlie. (*Tuts.*) Charlie's taken our Liam up to the hospital.

Laurence   Bastard!

Carol   Language! He never listens to a word I say.

She looks round at **Laurence**. *He's watching the telly. He realises she's just said something to him.*

Laurence   Sorry, what?

Carol   Take your feet off the table.

He ignores her.

Feet!

Laurence *takes his feet off the table.*

Carol   Did he tell you what he did today?

Laurence   What?

Carol   I'll leave him to tell you.

Laurence   What?

Carol   Oh, just something that's gonno affect each and every one of us in this house.

Laurence   Can we have something from the chippy for tea? I could just go a nice chiau su.

Carol   If you're paying.

Laurence   I give y'money every week, don't I?

Carol   Yeah, but a tenner every Friday doesn't stretch to chippy meals for four every Wednesday.

Laurence   It's not my fault you can't manage y'fuckin' money.

Carol   Don't you swear at me, y'cheeky little get!

Laurence   Ah, shut up.

Carol   Ay! What's got into you?

Terry *has come back in.*

Laurence   What's got into you more like! Just coz yer on y'jammy rag, don't take it out on me!

She smacks him round the head.

Carol   Your dad's packed work in. That's what's got into me.

Terry   Don't hit him, Carol.

Laurence   Don't lie! She's lyin', isn't she? Isn't she?

Terry *sits down.*

Laurence   Oh, fuckin'ell! That means we're not gonna get an 'oliday this year now.

Carol   That's right, Laurence, put everyone else before yourself as per friggin' usual.

Laurence   I hate that word, friggin'.

Pause. **Carol** *lights up a cigarette.*

Laurence   I thought we was goin' to Gran Canaria? Ah, this isn't on.

Terry   I'm sorry, lad.

Laurence   What d'you go and do that for, eh?

Terry   I couldn't hack it, lad.

Carol   Bollocks, you've been hacking it for nigh on ten years.

Laurence   Well, what we gonna do for an 'oliday?

Carol   Will you shut it, Laurence? There's more important things than holidays!

Laurence   Like what?

Carol (*smacks him over the head*)   If you wanna make yourself useful you can go and put some oven chips on.

Laurence (*jumps up*)   Yeah, well. Gotta line me stomach. I'm goin' out on the ale tonight. With me new bird.

He exits.

Carol   Not another one.

Terry   Don't hit him, Carol.

Carol   The way he speaks to me?

Terry   I'll talk to him.

Carol   Well, it's nice to know you'll talk to someone.

Pause.

Terry. What Marni was sayin' about the counselling.

Terry   No, Carol. No. Can you just leave it?

Carol   What were you knocking for Charlie for?

Terry   You're always on me fucking case.

Carol   You're not gonna get dole if you walked out the job.

Terry   I'll find something.

Carol   Get real, Terry.

Terry   I can't help the way I feel.

Carol   I'm gonna have to ask for extra hours at work. Thanks, Terry. Nice one.

Pause.

It'd be so easy. To pack a case and . . .

Terry   And what? Oh, you're gonna walk out on me now? Go on then. Prove to your mother she was right. I am a bad 'un. Rotten to the core. Well, it's true, isn't it? Isn't it?

Pause.

Carol   I'll give our Laurence an 'and wit the tea.

She gets up and goes out. **Terry** *sits there. The lights fade.*

Scene Three

The same, a few weeks later. **Liam** *is sitting watching an old film on the television. The front door goes and* **Laurence** *enters with his girlfriend* **Gina**. *They creep into the front room and are disappointed to find* **Liam** *there.* **Gina** *is dressed in red leggings and a red poncho with a red handbag and red boots. Her bizarre dress sense is quite appealing.*

Gina (*tuts*)   I thought you said . . .

Laurence   Shut up . . .

Gina   Ay! Don't tell me to shut up!

Laurence   Sorry, babes. (*To* **Liam**.) I thought you were going out wit y'mates?

Liam   They went swimming.

Gina   Couldn't you have gone wit them?

Liam   It's a free country, isn't it?

Laurence *sits down.* **Gina** *sits next to him.*

Laurence   Liam?

Liam *looks over.* **Laurence** *motions with his head to send him upstairs.*

Liam   What?

Laurence   Liam.

He motions him again.

Liam   You got a twitch?

Laurence   Get up them stairs now.

Liam   Oh, so yous two can eat face?

Gina   I'm sorry, Loll, but he's knockin' me sick.

Laurence   Liam!

Liam   Me ma said I can do what I like in this house.

Laurence   Oh, did she?

Liam   Yeah. Specially if yous two are around.

Laurence   Y'liar.

Liam   She did. Ask her if you don't believe me.

Laurence   I will.

Gina   I told you we shoulda gone to your room.

Laurence (*to* **Liam**)   Well, I'm tellin' you to move it.

Liam   I'm shitting me meself.

Gina   Oh, let's go upstairs, Loll.

Liam   Loll? (*Laughs.*)

Laurence   What's wrong wit Loll?

Liam   Nothing.

Pause.

Laurence   If Gina wants to call me Loll she can.

Gina   Laurence.

Laurence   We're staying here.

Gina   Let's go to your room.

Liam   Our room.

Laurence   My room.

Gina   Come on.

Pause.

Why not?

Liam   Coz it's got his crusty undies lying all over the floor.

Laurence *goes over and punches* **Liam**. **Liam** *hits him back.*
They start to fight. **Gina** *gets the remote control and messes around
with it. She lights up a ciggie as they fight. She doesn't take her eyes off
the TV.*

Gina   What's on the video? Jerry Springer? D'you like him?

Laurence *lays off the fighting and sits back next to* **Gina**.

Laurence   Do you?

Gina   There's nothing worse than seeing poor white trash fighting over crap.

Liam   Turn it off then.

Gina (*she doesn't*)   He's not a patch on Ricki Lake.

Laurence   Yeah, I know. I love Ricki Lake.

Gina   She's so good wit people. And she's lost so much weight. And she's just full o'so much love, and she'd never turn yer away if you were in trouble.

Liam   Mate o'yours, is she?

Gina   No, she's American. (*Yells at telly.*) Go on! Twat her! (*To* **Liam**.) So, you didn't fancy swimmin' then, no?

Laurence   He can't swim!

Gina   Can't yeh?

Liam   Yeah.

Laurence   Don't lie!

Liam   I can!

Laurence   Y'little spaz.

Liam   I'm not a spaz. I learned to swim at Butlin's. I've got a T-shirt with it on.

Laurence   You had your feet on the floor of the pool. You were walking round doing the breaststroke with yer hands and walking with yer feet. I seen yeh.

Liam   Well, how come they give me a T-shirt then?

Laurence   Coz you robbed it.

Gina   God, fancy robbin' a smelly arl T-shirt. Feel a cunt for yeh.

Liam   Shut up.

Laurence   Ay, that's my bird you're talking to.

Liam   Oh, goway, I thought it was Ricki Lake.

Laurence   D'you know you? Yer a spazzy and a queer.

Gina   Mm, I was on the bus last week. And we stopped at that stop over the road, and I looked over at this house, and I seen you . . . dancin' in your room.

Liam   How can I dance if I'm a spaz?

Laurence   Coz yer a queer an'all, and queer spazzies can dance.

Gina   I felt ashamed. I was the colour o'that. (*Points dramatically to her red poncho.*)

Liam   I was exercising.

Gina   You were all over the place.

Liam   Ah, I'm not talking to yous two.

Laurence   Good. Let's keep it that way, shall we?

The front doorbell goes.

Gina   God, it's like Spaghetti Junction in here!

Laurence   Liam. Liam. There's someone at the door.

Liam   Well, it's not gonna be for me, is it? All my mates have gone swimmin'.

Laurence   What, both of them?

Gina *laughs uproariously. The doorbell goes again.*

Liam   It's probably that girl you got pregnant last year. (**Gina** *stops laughing.*) Come for her maintenance.

Laurence (*to* **Gina**)   Take no notice. (*Gets up.*) D'you know you? Yer a spazzy, a queer . . . and a cunt. (*To* **Gina**.) Won't be long, babe.

He exits. **Liam** *pretends to vomit at his use of the word 'babe'.*

Gina   Yeah, well, if you were in love you'd call your girlfriend babe.

Liam   I thought I was a queer.

Gina   Well, yer fella then, Jesus. You wanna wake up and smell the coffee, Liam.

Liam   You wish what?

Gina   Speak the Queen's English, it's there for a purpose.

Laurence *enters with* **Marni**.

Laurence   I dunno where she is.

Liam   Me ma? She's gone shopping.

Marni   Hiya, Gina.

Gina   Hiya.

Marni   Still goin' strong, is it?

Liam   Yeah, more's the pity.

Gina   Laurence, I'm gonna deck him in a minute.

Marni   Is the kettle on, Laurence?

Laurence   Tea?

Marni   Please.

Laurence *exits*.

Gina   No sugar for me, I've got me sweeteners here.

Marni   Yer on a diet?

Gina   Yeah. It's the self same diet that helped Ricki Lake lose about thirty stone. I'll lend yer it if y'want.

Marni   Oh. Thanks.

Liam   Sit down, Marni.

Gina   I mean, have you seen her lately? You'd never guess it, would yer?

Marni   What?

Gina   Well, she used to be bigger than you. She used to be bigger than Scotland.

Pause.

Ah, how's that poor son o'yours?

Marni   Oh, you know.

Liam   He's in hospital.

Gina   Goway.

Marni   Out by the weekend hopefully.

Gina   Oh, well, isn't that fantastic? Oh, you must be over the moon, are yeh?

Marni   Well, I'll believe it when I see it.

Gina   Oh no. Them doctors know what they're talking about, you know. They do all sorts o'training. It's like a mental obstacle course to become a doctor these days. Have you never seen *Peak Practice*? What's he got again?

Marni   Cystic fibrosis.

Gina   No, d'you know what? That is a real coincidence, coz only last week, I seen them collecting for that up in town. Mm, I gave them twenny pee. Y'know.

Pause.

(*About the telly.*) I tell you what, Marni, he's not a patch on my Ricki.

Marni   No?

Gina   Is it fatal? Cystic fibrosis? It is, isn't it?

Marni   Well. There are cases where CF people have lived to old age.

Gina   CF?

Marni   Cystic fibrosis.

Gina   Oh, yeah. Oh, God, what am I like?!

Marni (*chuckles*)   It's not easy, you know.

Gina   I know. They had a show on *Ricki Lake* a few months ago now about children who were really ill with childhood illnesses. Did you see it?

Marni   No.

Gina   I tape it coz usually it's on when I'm at work. But oh my God, was I weeping buckets. People don't realise how difficult it is having a sick child, do they?

Marni   Well . . .

Gina   The issues involved are staggering.

Pause.

This is a good bit. The theme is I Wanna Come Out On National TV.

Pause.

Liam   Me mum should be back soon.

Marni   Oh, good, coz I've got some news.

Gina   Is it about your son?

Marni   Not really.

Liam   She's gone the Asda in Hunts Cross.

Marni   Has your dad driven her?

Liam   Nah, she was gettin' the bus.

Marni   Where is your dad?

Liam   Dunno. He's out though.

Gina (*about telly*)   State of him. I'm sorry, but Ricki wouldn't stand for that.

Marni   He's upset.

Gina   It's the parents I feel sorry for.

The front door goes.

Carol (*off*)   Is anyone in?

Liam *and* **Marni** *get up.*

Liam/Marni   Yeah!!

Gina   In here, Carol!

Carol (*off*)   Someone give me an 'and with your dad.

Liam *goes off.* **Marni** *follows.* **Gina** *is left on her own watching the telly.* **Liam** *and* **Carol** *bring a very drunken* **Terry** *in.* **Marni** *follows.*

Carol   Get him on the couch.

Gina   Oh my God, what's the matter with him? Is he all right?

Liam   He reeks o'booze.

Marni   Where did you find him?

Carol   In the car.

They lie him down on the couch. **Gina** *stands and carries on watching the telly.*

Lying on the back seat of his fucking car.

Gina   I didn't think he could drive.

Liam   Yeah he can.

Gina   Goway.

Marni   Gina, would you put Carol's shopping away? It's all on the step.

Gina   Oh. Oh, OK then. Can I just see this?

She stands watching the telly, mouthing the words. She smiles then moves off.

(*To* **Terry**.) What are you like, eh?

She exits.

Marni   What was he doin' in the car?

Carol   He hadn't been drivin' it. He was just asleep in it.

Marni   Take the weight off your feet. Liam, get another cuppa going for your mum.

Liam *exits*.

Carol   I'm sick of it, Marni.

Marni   D'you want a ciggie?

Carol (*takes one*)   I'm walking round that fucking supermarket with a calculator. Adding it all up so's I don't go over me budget. And where's he? Getting langing drunk in the pub. I dunno where he gets the money from.

Marni   He's a popular lad. Everyone gets the ale in for Terry.

Carol   He's not popular here. I went past the pub the other day. Have I told you this? (**Marni** *shakes her head as she lights* **Carol**'s *cigarette*.) And I just glimpsed through the window. And I seen him. And he was just a totally different person. Laughing and joking wit the footy crowd. I was stood there with me nose right up against the glass. It was pouring with rain. I must've looked a right prat.

Marni   And who looks a prat now?

Carol   Why's he like this, Marni? Why's he a different person here to the way he is out there?

Marni   He hasn't got to put on an act for you.

Carol   Him and his fuckin' football. I've tried, Marni. I have.

Marni   I know, love.

Carol   I've tried to understand. To be patient. To give it time. But how long does he need? Every fucking April without fail he just sinks down. And he won't talk to me about it.

Marni   Sit down, darling.

Carol   I can't go on like this.

Marni   You've got to.

Carol   Have I?

Gina *enters with a tub of ice cream.*

Gina   Oh, have you tried this? Too Good To Be True? Oh, it's marvellous this. It's like all the taste of ice cream, with hardly any fat. Should I ladle some out for everyone? Oh, go on, Carol. I think you need to take a swim in Lake You.

Carol (*shrugs*)   Whatever.

Gina   You know it makes sense.

Gina *exits.*

Marni   A marriage is for life, Carol.

Carol   How's your Wayne?

Marni   Not too good. Out by the weekend, so they say. But I think he looks shocking. I can't stay too long. I wanna get up there and take over from Charlie's mum.

Carol   Oh, get off now, Marni, d'you want me to come with you?

Marni   No. No.

Laurence *enters with their teas.*

Laurence   Ay, Mam. You can't lend us a tenner, can yeh? I promised Gina I'd take her the karaoke tonight and I'm brassic.

Carol No, Laurence, I can't.

Laurence Don't suppose you could, Marni.

Carol No she couldn't. I dunno where your money goes to.

Laurence God, I only asked.

Carol If you want karaoke, put the stereo on and sing along to it.

Laurence Has me dad got any money?

Marni I think he's drunk every last penny, lad.

Laurence He might have.

Carol *slams down her tea and goes over to* **Terry** *who is fast asleep on the couch. She rifles through his pockets. He groans.*

Carol Oh, well, let's see, shall we? Terry? Your son wants a tenner. No? You got anything left? Come on, empty your pockets out, lad. Oh, nothing for our Laurence? Oh, you do surprise me. Oh, hang on. (*She goes in her handbag.*)

Laurence All right, Ma.

Carol Let's see how much we've got here. (*Empties her bag on to the chair.*)

Laurence I said all right.

Carol Seventy-five? No! Seventy-eight pence. Oh, well, I think we can all go the karaoke on that.

Gina *enters with* **Liam**, *carrying two trays of ice cream.*

Gina Karaoke? Oh, are we's all going? Oh, yeah it'll be a laugh that. Oh, I love the karaoke me. Dunno what I'm going to sing.

Marni Try 'Beg Steal Or Borrow'.

Gina (*offering ice cream*)   Too Good To Be True?

Carol Try 'Ticket To Ride'.

Gina   Oh, I'll let you OAPs do the golden oldies. I'm gonna do something bang up to date. Laurence?

Laurence   Tar.

Gina   Oh, don't I get a babe now?

Laurence   Bad news, babe. Karaoke's off.

Gina   Oh, Loll, you promised.

Laurence   I know.

Gina   Oh, Loll, I was looking forward to that.

Laurence   I'm sorry, babe.

Gina   Oh, why?

Carol   Coz he's skint!

Gina   Skint?

Carol   Are you deaf?

Gina   I lent you thirty quid last night.

Pause.

Liam   What's your good news, Marni?

Gina   I didn't wanna say before, but I have been practising 'What Will She Look Like With A Chimney On Her?' for weeks.

Liam   Have you told her?

Marni   No.

Gina   And if they didn't have that I was gonna do the theme from *Titanic* and dedicate it to you.

Carol   What, Marni?

Laurence   I'll make it up to yeh.

Gina   If it's not karaoke it's McDonald's. You're always letting me down.

Liam   Will you just shut up for once in your life, eh?
Marni's got something to tell me mum.

Gina   God, you can't open your mouth in this house.

Carol (*shouts*)   Well, if you don't like it you know what you
can do, don't yeh?! Fuck off back to Fazackerly!!

Gina (*almost in tears*)   I'm not from Fazackerly.

Pause. **Gina** *is belittled by the roar from* **Carol**. *She slips on to the
arm of a chair.*

Carol   Marni?

Blackout.

Scene Four

The same, that night. **Terry** *sits up on the couch nursing an Alka
Seltzer.* **Carol** *comes in in her dressing-gown and starts putting some
washing out to dry on a clothes horse at the back of the room. She stares
at him as she does this.*

Terry   Are the kids in bed?

Carol   Liam is.

Terry   Laurence?

Carol   Gone to Otterspool Prom with Gina.

Pause.

Otterspool Prom. Take you back?

Terry   Me head.

Carol   I hope they're not doing what we used to do there.

Terry   What time is it?

Carol   You were in the car.

Terry   The car?

Carol   Back seat.

Terry   Liverpool won. The lads were celebrating.

Carol   I've never seen you like that.

Terry   I hadn't eaten.

Carol   I think we should take up Marni's offer.

Pause.

A free holiday.

Terry   It's not Gran Canaria.

Carol   No. And it's not here either. I think it'd do us some good.

Terry   I dunno.

Carol   I do.

She kneels at his feet and kisses him.

Terry   Me breath.

Carol   Doesn't matter.

She kisses him again.

Bed?

Pause.

We could just cuddle.

Terry   You go up. I'll be up in a sec.

Carol *gets up. She goes to the door and looks back at him.*

Carol   You've got no fight left in yeh.

Terry   Eh?

Pause.

Carol   Night.

Terry   Carol?

Carol Well, look at yeh! Sat in that seat while the world passes you by. I used to love you coz you were a fucking fighter.

Terry What you tryina say?

Carol Don't you dare twist my words, Terry Fitzgibbon, you know I still love you. Christ, would I put up with this if I didn't?

Terry What you talking about, Carol?

Carol Fifteen we were. Our Liam's age when we went down to Otterspool Prom. And when I got pregnant, what did we do? We fought. We fought your mam and dad and my mam and everyone on that street who said we were too fucking young. Gymslip mother, only a baby herself! When they wanted to send me away we fought. Have an abortion. We fought. Christ, when I got called for all sorts in the school playground you went round hammering the bastards who'd called me names.

Terry Where's this coming from?

Carol (*punching her heart*) From here! And when we had our little baby we were the happiest kids on the street, but we had to keep on fighting. When we ran away to Scotland and you made a decent woman of me, I walked back down our street with me head held high. We got the little flat, then this little house and another fucking baby and it was one long fight.

Terry Are you saying we should have got rid of our Laurence?

Carol No! No! I just want to know what's wrong with you, Terry. Have you fought so much that you've got nothing left? Coz I find it hard. To keep it up. But the one thing I never had to fight was you.

Terry I don't wanna fight with you, Carol.

Carol   But I do! I need you to fight now, you bastard. Fight for us. For something. Was it not worth it? Were they?

Terry   How can you say that?

Pause.

Carol   Oh, always this fucking silence. Well, maybe you'll have to find some fight in you soon. Coz our baby's down Otterspool Prom now with some slip of a girl and history has a habit of repeating itself.

Terry   He's not daft.

Carol   No. And neither were we. But I don't fancy being a grandma when I've not even seen thirty-five.

Terry   You don't think . . .

Carol   One day soon, Terry. The kids'll have gone. And then it'll just be us. The last time it was just us, Terry, we were still at school. What are we gonna be like now? With you not speaking and me treading on eggshells.

Terry   They won't go just yet.

Carol   I'm gonna go on this holiday. I'm gonna take the kids and we're gonna go. It'd be nice, for them, if you came as well. We'll have our own caravan, Terry. And in the next one'll be Marni, Charlie and their Wayne.

Terry   I love you, Carol.

She's frustrated by his lack of response.

Carol   I'm gonna take me make-up off.

Carol *exits.* **Terry** *sits there. He gets up and puts the light off and goes and sits down again, drinking his Alka Seltzer. The front door goes. The hall light goes on and* **Laurence** *and* **Gina** *come in and close the door, snogging at the back of the room.* **Terry** *watches, not knowing what to do with himself.* **Laurence** *pushes* **Gina** *against the back wall to kiss her. Her head bangs against the light switch and the light comes on. They see* **Terry** *sitting there.*

Gina   Ah me head!!

Laurence   Oh, oright, Dad?

Terry   I'm just off to bed.

Gina   Oh, God, I bet you've got a hangover and a half. Is yer head pulsating?

Terry   Something like that.

Gina   Night, Terry.

Terry   Yeah. Night, girl.

He exits.

Gina   It was Christmas Eve and all in the house there wasn't a sound, not even a mouse.

Laurence   Apart from your big fucking hole.

She sits on the couch.

Gina   You wish what?

Laurence   D'you wanna Bacardi?

Gina   No.

Laurence   I'm having one.

He gets a bottle from the sideboard and pours one.

Anyway, it's not Christmas Eve.

Gina   Goway. Ah, aren't yer excited?

Laurence   What about?

Gina   This holiday. I know I am.

Laurence   Why?

Gina   I think it's marvellous.

Laurence   I don't know whether me ma'll let you come.

Gina   I'm your girlfriend, aren't I? I always go on holiday wit me boyfriends.

Laurence   You don't wanna go to Wales, Gina. A caravan site.

Gina   You mean *you* don't want me to go.

Laurence   I didn't say that.

Gina   There might be a forest in Tenby.

Laurence   So?

Gina   If you could lose your virginity again, where would it be?

Laurence   Er, again? Dunno.

Gina   I do.

Laurence   Where?

Gina   In a forest.

Laurence   You mean . . .

Gina   Best yer have a word wit yer ma.

Laurence   I bet there's loads o'forests in Tenby.

Gina   I know.

Laurence *comes and sits next to her.*

Gina   Oh, isn't that a beautiful clothes maiden?

Laurence   Gina.

Gina   My mum just puts things on the radiator.

Laurence   I don't wanna drink this from the glass. I wanna drink it from you.

Gina   Y'what?

Laurence   Go on.

Gina   All right but make it quick. I don't wanna miss me last bus.

She takes a swig of the Bacardi. She keeps it in her mouth then kisses him, transferring the Bacardi to his mouth. He swallows it.

Laurence   I can't wait for Tenby.

She repeats the process.

Gina   Where did your mother get that clothes maiden?

Laurence   Dunno.

Gina   One more and that's your lot.

Laurence   I could find out for you.

As they do a Bacardi kiss the phone rings.

Gina   It's a bit late for phone calls, isn't it?

Laurence *gets up and answers the phone.*

Laurence   Hello? No, she's in bed. So's he. Are you all right, Marni?

Pause.

Jesus Christ.

Pause.

Yeah, I'll tell 'em. Where are yeh now? They'll probably wanna come. Oh, OK. Fine. Jesus, Marni. OK. Trar.

He puts the phone down. Pause.

Gina   Marni?

Laurence   It's their Wayne.

Gina   It's not what I'm thinking, is it?

Laurence *(nods his head)*   I've got to tell me mum.

Gina   D'you want me to do it?

Laurence *(shakes his head)*   You go for your bus.

Gina   Are you sure?

Laurence   I'll see yer in work.

Gina   I could make cups o'tea.

Laurence *shakes his head.*

Gina   How old was he?

Laurence   Same as our Liam.

Gina   See you tomorrow.

Laurence   I'll walk you to the stop.

Gina   It's only across the way.

She kisses him.

Trar.

Laurence   Trar.

Gina *leaves.* **Laurence** *pours another Bacardi and lights a fag.*

Carol (*off*)   Who was that on the phone?!

Laurence   Er . . . Marni!

Carol (*off*)   What's the matter?!

Laurence   Stay there, I'm coming up.

Carol (*off*)   Laurence?!

Laurence *knocks back the Bacardi, stubs the ciggie out and exits. The lights fade.*

Scene Five

The back garden.

A week later, **Terry** *and* **Charlie** *sit drinking, in funeral gear. Cans litter the coffee table. They're smoking.* **Charlie**'s *more pissed than* **Terry**. *From next door, the sounds of a party.* **Liam** *comes in in his school uniform.*

Terry   Oright, son?

Liam   Me mam sent me.

Terry   Oh aye?

Liam   She said when are yous thinking of coming back over?

Terry   When Charlie's ready.

Liam   Can I have a swig o'that?

Terry *hands him the can.* **Liam** *has a swig.*

Terry   We'll make a man of you yet.

Liam   Tar.

Terry   Is everyone still there?

Liam   Yeah. I'll get back to the do.

Liam *exits.*

Charlie   D'you think your Liam's a puff?

Terry   Y'what? Liam?

Pause.

He's a big girl's blouse but he's fuckin' sound.

Charlie   D'yer ever think Carol dotes on him a bit much?

Terry   I dote on him more than her. She's dead strict with him.

Charlie   Our fuckin' Marni. Doted on Wayne. Spoilt him rotten. The lad never heard the word no from her. Can't blame her like. But. He was never gonna be a man. I seen it from the word go. Knew it. I just knew. You can't hurt a sick kid but. Oh, Terry, I loved him. You know that, don't yeh?

Terry   You fuckin' idolised that lad.

Charlie   I did. I did. Bloody . . . going to violin lessons. Violin? The happiest I ever saw him was when he got *My Fair Lady* out the video library. It's not right, is it?

Terry   Ay, it won a shitload of Oscars.

Charlie   He was never into all that rave music. I was more into it than him. Sitting in his room listening to all the old songs off the tapes his grandma had made him. She had him sussed. When I'd put me music on he'd be like, 'Dad. Turn it down. Three hundreds beats a minute and no tune.' Sometimes I thought he was a bird in a lad's body but. (*Shrugs.*)

Terry   Ay, he was a crackin' kid.

Charlie   I know.

Terry   You idolised him.

Charlie   I know.

Terry   Ay.

Charlie   What?

Terry   He was all right.

Pause.

Kids are gifts to us, Charlie.

Charlie   Death doesn't scare me.

Terry   After all . . . that little lad. When we . . . I could tell he was a young lad coz of his voice. Shouting for his mam. Me foot was on his chest. I couldn't see him. Then the safety barrier went and we all ended up on top of him. The life squoze out of him. Don't be funny about your Wayne, when . . . that poor fucking kid.

Charlie   I hate meself, Terry.

Terry   Your Wayne was all right.

Charlie   It was Marni that made him like that.

Terry   Ay, she only done what she thought was best for the lad. I'm the same.

Charlie   No, you're not.

Terry   I am.

Charlie   I don't hate you.

Pause.

Terry   You're bevvied.

Pause.

I climbed over some arl fella's shoulders to get out that cage. Hands lifting me over. And the first things I heard was our Liam's voice. 'I've lost me dad.' Screaming. I turned round and he's there with this busy. It took thirty-three minutes to find our Laurence. Kept lookin' at me watch. Felt like for ever. Lying on the pitch. He'd pissed and shat hisself. I got them home, back here. And all Carol could do was say. 'I told you. I told you they were too young for an away game.' Eight and six.

Charlie   You were lucky. Try to get our Wayne interested in the match and he'd laugh in your face.

Terry   We'd had such a battle to have them in the first place and then that. I'm sorry, Char.

Charlie   You don't know how lucky yer are.

Terry   I don't care what they are. I've got 'em. Don't be angry with your Marni. Be angry with the cunt up there who lets this happen.

Pause. **Liam** *enters again.*

Liam   Me mam says she wants you to come over.

Charlie   We're not ready yet, Liam.

Terry   Liam.

He hugs **Liam** *to him.* **Liam** *wrestles away.*

Liam   Are y'gonna come?

Terry   Soon.

Liam *exits.* **Charlie** *is crying.*

Charlie   Oh fuckin'ell. I never cry.

Terry   You're a top fella, Charlie.

Charlie   I hate . . . I haven't felt like this since Hillsborough. It's brought it all back. The nightmares. Just when I thought I was over it. I know I'm a twat.

Terry   I don't give a shit about you cryin', Char.

Charlie   Well, I do.

Pause.

It's not Wayne's fault.

Pause.

Three weeks ago. That day I took them machines over to New Brighton. Our Marni made us a packed lunch. I'm eating it on the front there. Top day. And there's this girl on the next bench down. Dirty, y'know. Smackhead. And she's got this mini-skirt on. And she's spreading her legs. Looking over. And I'm getting turned on.

Pause.

I shagged her in the back of the van and give her ten quid. Said her name was Donna. She was sixteen.

Pause.

A dirty fuck. I dunno what's happening to me.

Terry   Stress.

Charlie   I don't suppose you've ever . . . (**Terry** *shakes his head.*) I can get a hard-on just thinking about it.

Terry   I thought everything was OK wi' yous two.

Charlie   OK? Yeah it's OK. But OK's not, you know. I'm not leaving her or anything like that, Te'. Don't fret. Nah, stuck with the fat bitch now. If I could get out I would. But. Ah, never mind.

Pause.

I feel better for that.

Terry   Yeah. Don't take it out on your Wayne.

Charlie   There's so many evil cunts around. Why couldn't it've happened to them lads that killed Jamie Bulger?

Terry   I dunno.

Charlie   I gotta get away, Terry. I need a break, mate.

Terry   There's always Tenby.

Charlie   You know I hate the fresh air. Marni's brother said I could go and work with him if I wanted.

Terry   In London?

Charlie   Do four days a week down there and back here for weekends. Col's a foreman. Hires and fires. Always said no up 'til now on account of hospital trips. But now.

Terry   Doesn't Marni mind? (**Charlie** *shrugs.*) I think she will, y'know.

Charlie   I wouldn't do it for long.

Terry   She needs you now.

Charlie   Women are good copers.

Terry   Bullshit.

Charlie   Look at your Carol.

Terry   What about our Carol?

Charlie   Well, she's had to cope with you and all that for . . . nine years now. She doesn't need that. But she's got it, and she's coping. I mean, when was the last time you and her . . . ?

Pause.

I'm being way outa line here, Te'. It's none o'my business. She talks to Marni about it and you know Marni. Forever going on.

Terry   At least I don't have to go looking for it somewhere else. Like New fucking Brighton.

Charlie   Ah come on, Te'. We're mates.

Terry   I know like, y'know. But. Ay, you don't think she's . . . ?

Charlie   Carol? No.

Terry   No.

Charlie   She'da told Marni.

Terry   Ay, this if off its chunk.

Charlie   You'd be able to tell.

Pause.

Women cope with whatever you throw at them. If I do just two weeks in London, in me time off from work. She can go to Tenby, I can make a nice bit o'cash and get a break all into the bargain. Ay, you could come an'all.

Terry   Ah no.

Charlie   Col'd take yer on for a fortnight.

Terry   Nah, I couldn't. Carol's really looking forward to Tenby.

Charlie   Women love nothing better than getting rid o'their arl fellas for a few days.

Terry   Two weeks?

Charlie   Even better. She'd have Marni there.

Terry   I know but.

Charlie   It's not Carol, is it?

Terry   What?

Charlie   It's you.

Terry   Me?

Charlie   Ah no, Te'. I understand like.

Terry   What?

Charlie   You're like, agoraphobic an' all that.

Terry   I'm not.

Charlie   Forget it, Te'. I'll go on me own.

Terry   I'm not an agoraphobic. I'm not.

Charlie   S'all right, Te'. I've been there.

Terry   But I'm not.

Charlie   Ah, but think about it. You in London? A city you don't know? The pace? The people? Tubes an' all that? Nah, Te'. You wouldn't hack it.

Pause.

Terry   We should be gettin' back.

Charlie   Ay, don't say nothing to *her*, will yeh?

Terry   I won't.

Pause.

Where would you stay?

Charlie   In London? Colin's pad. It's massive.

Terry   And there'd definitely be a job?

Charlie   I've told yer, haven't I? Why?

Terry   Nothing. I'm pissed.

Marni *comes in wearing a black dress. She tidies away their lager cans.*

Marni   Charlie. Y'mam's givin' me all sorts o'grief in there. Keeps askin' where yer are.

Charlie   We're comin' now.

Marni   His teacher's pissed. Crying her eyes out in the corner. I could do without that.

Charlie   Come on, Terry lad. Time we faced the music.

Marni   Your Liam's being an angel. Filling everyone's drink up.

Terry   Yeah, well. He's a good kid. Wayne was his best mate.

Charlie   Ay! Marni Sweet!

Marni   What, Three-Piece?

Charlie *gets up and sings to her, holding his can aloft. He starts to sing 'My Special Angel' by Malcolm Vaughan.*

He stops singing.

Marni (*upset*)   You soft prick. That was his song.

She exits.

Terry   See? You can't help but love her, can you?

Charlie *shrugs and the tears pour.* **Terry** *doesn't know what to do. Eventually he stands up and hugs* **Charlie** *to him. The lights fade.*

Scene Six

The lounge.

A few weeks later. **Carol** *is hoovering.* **Terry** *is reading* **Liam**'s *school report.* **Liam** *is spark out on the couch.* **Carol** *is looking at him. She switches the Hoover off. The telly and video have disappeared.*

Carol   Listen to him, he's snoring.

Terry   PE . . . F! Hard to comment. Liam never brings correct kit and is sullen and uncooperative when forced to participate. That can't be true!

Carol   You'll have to have a word with Mrs Raymond. She can find someone else to walk her dog so late.

Terry   He loves sport.

The doorbell goes. **Liam** *wakes up.* **Carol** *looks out of the window.*

You love games.

Liam   What?

Carol   Get the door, it's Marni.

Terry   Footy. The match.

Carol   Terry.

Terry   What?

Carol (*now* **Liam***'s gone out*)   He hates games.

Terry   Don't be daft.

Enter **Marni**. *She has an apron on. She stands there.*

Carol   Hiya, love. Oh, God, is it all getting a bit on top of you?

Marni   Yer haven't got a ciggie, have yeh?

Carol   Sit down.

Marni   I've come out without me Consulate.

Carol   Terry, pass us . . . tar.

Marni   Tar.

Carol *is signalling for* **Terry** *to get out.*

Terry   Think I'll put the kettle on.

Marni   I think you better stay, Terry. This involves you.

Carol   What's happened?

Marni   Oh, I'm standing there, in the back kitchen, putting his tea on. I'm just cracking an egg and watching it sizzle nicely in the pan, when he drops the most massive, almightiest clanger I've ever heard in me life.

Carol   Charlie?

Marni   Only reckons he's not going to Tenby.

Carol   What?

Marni   Oh no. Reckons him and Terry here are going off to London for a fortnight to work for our Colin.

Carol   What?

Marni   Oh, so Terry hasn't told you?

Carol   Terry?

Terry   It's nothing definite.

Carol   Say that again.

Marni   Charlie and Terry aren't coming to Tenby. They're going to do two weeks in London helping my brother do up some toff's mansion.

Carol   No. No! This is . . . it's stupid.

Marni   It's more than stupid, it's fucking ridiculous.

The doorbell goes.

Carol   But . . .

Terry   I didn't say I would.

Marni   Tell me it's just another of Charlie's hare-brain schemes. Pie in the sky. Like when he was gonna buy that plot of land and turn it into a city zoo.

Terry   He'll come to Tenby. You'll see.

Enter **Charlie**.

Charlie (*to* **Marni**)   Ay, you, the tea's ruined.

Marni   Oh, piss off, you, cunt.

Charlie   Well, that's the pot calling the kettle black.

Carol   Don't you wanna come to Tenby, Charlie?

Charlie   Of course I wanna come to Tenby.

Carol   Well, that's settled then.

Charlie   It's just . . .

Marni   See?

Charlie   It's just, you know. I'm not one for holidays, you know that. The only reason we was getting that caravan in the first place was to give Wayne a nice break.

Marni   It was very kind of our Colin to give us his caravan for the fortnight.

Charlie   But now Wayne's not here . . .

Marni   Oh, but your wife doesn't need a break, does she? I'll just sit in staring at the four walls like something out of *One Flew Over the Cuckoo's Nest*.

Charlie   I know you need a break. I'm not daft.

Marni   Imagine how I'd feel in a caravan all on me own knowing our Wayne was supposed to be there an'all.

Charlie   I just thought. Oh, forget it. Come on, you.

Carol   What? What did you think?

Charlie   I know things is hard for you and Terry. Not working. It just seemed ideal to take up Col's offer.

Marni (*to* **Carol**)   Will you listen to that? Mother Fucking Teresa of Calcutta's godson. (*To* **Charlie**.) Col doesn't offer a thing unless you put it into his head. The extra caravan for this lot was your idea. Christ, you think more of Terry than you do me.

Carol   And it's a nice thought, Charlie, but . . . you can't leave Marni on her own. Not now.

Charlie   I realise that. I do. Come on, you. I'm hungry.

Marni   You're not getting so much as a Pot Noodle out o'me tonight.

Charlie   Come 'ed, girl. I'll cook.

Marni   I'm not that keen on salmonella and chips tar, babe.

Charlie   Now who's being unreasonable? I've said I'll come to Tenby. We both will, won't we, Te'?

Terry   Yeah.

Pause.

Marni   Go to London. See if I care. If that's what you want, go! I don't want you hangin' round a perfectly good caravan for a fortnight if you don't wanna be there.

Carol   Marni, you don't mean that.

Marni   D'you wanna bet?

Charlie   No. I'll ring Col. Tell him to call it off.

Marni   Don't try and make me feel guilty.

Charlie   Snap.

Marni   I've done nothing wrong.

Marni *gets up.*

Charlie   Where you goin'?

Marni   The toilet. Why? D'you wanna wipe me arse?

She exits.

Charlie   I'm sorry about this, Carol. We'll get outa your way in a minute.

Carol   Terry. Did you wanna go to London?

Terry   No.

Charlie   Oh, cheers, mate.

Terry   Well, I don't now.

Carol   You'd actually go down there. And work?

Terry   Ah, forget it, Carol.

Carol   Forget it? I'm fascinated.

Terry   I got us into this mess. I thought I could try and get us out.

Carol   I don't believe you sometimes.

Terry   I reckon I'd be all right with Charlie.

Charlie   Carol. We're looking at the best part of a grand for two weeks' work. Now you can't knock that, can yeh?

Carol   I don't believe you either. Just upping and leaving Marni so soon after Wayne.

Charlie   I hate having time to meself. I need to keep going. Take me mind off things. If I have too much time on me hands I go on a downer. I know that coz o'the counselling. I'm being dead selfish, I know. But, me and Marni's different in that respect. If I have two weeks with her with nothing to do, she'll wanna keep goin' on about Wayne, and . . . I know she needs that, but . . . I'd rather not think about it.

Marni's *come back to the doorway. He's not seen her.*

Charlie   I know I'm being selfish, but I just wanno hang on to me sanity. I've lost that once. I don't wanna lose it again.

Marni *is crying.* **Liam** *comes to the door and puts his arm around her.*

Liam   You all right, Marni?

Marni   You can say it to them but you can't say it to me.

Charlie   If you'd given me time I would. But you came storming round here. I thought you were goin' the loo.

Marni   There's no toilet paper.

Carol   Isn't there? Oh bloody'ell.

Marni   It's all right. I can hang on 'til I get home.

Carol   Oh, for God's sake. We're living off beans on toast. We've sent the TV and video back today. And now there's no bog roll. I'll have to go the shop. Terry, have you got a couple o'quid?

Terry *shakes his head.*

Carol   No?

Charlie   Eeyar, Carol.

Carol   Liam?

Charlie   Carol . . . (*He's holding out some money.*)

Carol   It's OK.

Liam   In me piggy bank.

Carol   Will you get it?

Liam *exits.*

Terry   I'm sorry, Carol. I'm sorry, Marni.

Marni   Ay, Carol. How d'you fancy sharing a caravan with me? Give the kids one to themselves?

Carol *sighs desperately, then throws her head back and starts to laugh.* **Marni** *joins in, shaking her head. The doorbell goes.*

Liam (*off*)   I'll get it!

Carol   If it's Christian Aid, rob the buggers!

She and **Marni** *laugh.* **Gina** *enters with* **Liam** *who is carrying his piggy bank.* **Gina** *is dressed head to toe in turquoise; leggings, boots, poncho and Alice band. She carries a video cassette and a newspaper.*

Gina   Hiya! Hiya, Marni, ah. Laurence not back yet no?

Carol   No, love.

Gina   Oh, it's nice to see you having a giggle, Marni, love. Takes more muscles to frown than to smile you know. Now, does anyone mind if I watch this afternoon's *Ricki Lake* 'til he gets back? I'll only have it on quiet, only I haven't had a chance to watch it yet, and you know what I'm like.

Carol   Feel free, go right ahead.

Gina   I know yous all think I'm stupid.

Carol   Well, you can't be more stupid than us.

Gina   Oh, I can't wait for Tenby, you know. Us girls are gonna have a right giggle. I had this dream the other night. And us three were sitting round a camp fire, just pissing ourselves. I couldn't get over it. Video.

She moves to where the telly usually is. She sees it's gone.

Oh.

Liam   Mum?

Liam *has got a couple of pounds out of his piggy bank.*

Marni   Give it him back. Gina? Could I borrow your paper?

Gina   Sure, Marni, yeah, you go right ahead. We're gonna have to get used to share and share alike when we're on our hols!

Carol   It's a caravan we're going to, you know, not the friggin' outback.

Gina   Oh, you know what I mean, Carol.

Marni   Any particular section you don't like, Gina?

Gina   Telly reviews. They've been slagging my Ricki, cunts.

They all giggle at her turn of phrase. **Marni** *takes the paper and goes to exit to the loo with it.*

Marni   Well, if it was good enough for my arl girl in the war, it's good enough for me!

She exits. **Carol** *starts to laugh again. Eventually her laughter turns
to tears.* **Liam** *goes and hugs her. He starts crying too.* **Terry** *and*
Charlie *look fed up.*

Gina   Oh, listen stop it. Oh, will yous stop it?

They keep crying.

God feel ashamed for yous.

Terry *stars to cry.*

Gina   What are yous like?! Smile, kidders, it might never
happen!

Liam   Shut up, will yeh.

Gina   Are yous all mad or something? We're going on our
holidays!! Jesus.

She sits down on the arm of the chair. Just then **Laurence** *comes in.
He sees everyone crying.*

Gina   Don't look at me.

Laurence   I got a taxi back. Can anyone lend us a
tenner?

Blackout.

Act Two

Scene One

A forest in Tenby.

Pitch black and approaching midnight, there is just a hint of moonlight shining down through the trees. **Laurence** *enters shining a torch ahead of him.* **Gina** *follows him eating chips. She wears a yellow poncho, leggings and platform trainers. She is trying to eat, but can't see where she is going.*

Gina Laurence!

Laurence Com 'ed.

Gina I've got platform trainees on, I'm gonna go arse over tit.

He shines the torch so she can see where she is going.

Up here. I can't see me chips.

He shines the torch so she can see her food. They stop where they are.

I'm having to force these down. Christ knows how much weight I'm going to put on.

He puts his hand between her legs. She slaps him off.

Do I look really fat?

Laurence Huge.

Gina Do I?

Laurence No.

Gina Best I get on that *Ricki Lake*. I'll be sat on that chair and on the screen it'll say 'Gina: She's ballooned.'

Laurence I'll have to go an'all.

Gina Yeah?

Laurence And it'll say 'Laurence: His knob is aching.'

Gina   Ricki wouldn't stoop so low.

Laurence   It's only when you're around.

Gina   Mm, well, I'll be very around if I'm eating chips every night. You'll have to spin me round to get out the house. Can't believe it.

Laurence   What's got into you?

Gina   Fat's a feminist issue, gobshite.

Laurence   And I can't help being a man, with a man's needs.

Gina   God, you're obsessed, you.

Laurence   You have this effect on me, Gina.

Gina   God, if I had a pound for every time someone had said that to me.

Laurence   You'd be fuckin' skint.

Gina   I'd be as rich as Ricki.

Laurence   Will you stop goin' on about her?

Gina   Well, you stop goin' on about y'knob then.

Laurence   So who else's said it to you?

Gina   Everyone. Jammed up against the bus shelter aged thirteen with some big fat hairy monster from the youth club tryina stick it between me legs . . . 'You have this effect on me, Gina.' Bending over the photocopier at work: 'Photocopy this, love.' 'Fuck off, Phil.' 'But Gina, you have this effect on me!'

Laurence   Phil who?

Gina   I've seen more erections than a master scaffolder. I'm sick of it.

Laurence   Phil who? Who said that at work?

Gina   It was before I was transferred to your branch.

Laurence   I'll fuckin' deck him.

Gina   Deck yourself, you're all the same.

Laurence   Is that why you were moved to our branch?

Gina   I kicked him in the bollocks with me Spice Girl trainees and the bastard put in a grievance procedure.

Laurence   Sit down.

Gina   I'm not sitting down there, the filth of it!

Laurence *takes his coat off and spreads it on the floor.*

Laurence   Madam?

She sits down on his coat. He remains standing.

But I'm allowed to say it to yeh, coz I'm your fella.

Gina   I'm gonna kill you if we're lost.

Laurence   Aren't I?

Gina   And don't be whipping nothing out.

Laurence   We're not lost.

Gina   Well, where are we then?

Laurence   Caravan's about ten minutes that way.

Gina   How do you know?

Laurence   Coz look up there.

They look up into the sky.

Gina   Mm?

Laurence   They're the exact same stars that y'see from the caravan.

Gina (*tuts*)   They're the exact same stars you can see from my bedroom window at home. What do you know about stars?

Laurence   I know where we are.

Gina   Well, what's that one called? The big bright fuck-off one at the top.

Laurence   That's the guiding star.

Gina   The what? Never heard of it.

Laurence   So me dad says.

Gina   Your dad? And you believe him? Feel a cunt for yeh.

Laurence   I can believe him if I want.

Gina   And I suppose you believe that there's fairies at the bottom of the garden. Stars don't have names like that, Laurence. They have names like 'The Plough' and 'The Bear' and 'Orion's Belt'. Guiding star me arse.

Laurence   My dad said if yer ever got lost, you could look up into the sky and one of two things would happen.

Gina   Surprise me.

Laurence   You'd either see one of the Liver Birds off the Liver Buildings flying in the sky, and it'd fly back to Liverpool so's you could follow it.

Gina   Or?

Laurence   Or you'd see that bright star, the guiding star, that'd get yeh home, coz it shines right above our house.

Gina   Who does he think you are? Jesus?

Laurence   I like it.

Gina   Your dad's soft in the head, it's common knowledge.

Laurence   No he's not.

Gina   And as for that mother o'yours. She was the one who said I could share a caravan with you and your Liam in the first place. But you shoulda seen the daggers she give me this morning when I comes out the caravan in me nightie.

Like we'd been shaggin' in front of your Liam. I felt ay-fuckin'-shamed.

Laurence   No danger o'that with your attitude.

Gina   I can't help being on me period.

Laurence   I don't mind, you know.

Gina   Good. Coz I never come away to have sex wit yer, Loll. I came away to have valuable time wit yeh.

Laurence   No. I don't *mind*.

Gina   What?

Laurence   A bit o'blood.

Gina   Y'know, you?

Laurence   What?

Gina   Y'dead romantic.

Laurence   D'y'reckon?

Gina   Well, put it this way, if I was on *Ricki Lake* now it'd say 'Gina: She's bein' sarky.'

Laurence   I dunno why you bothered comin'.

Gina   I've told you why. This is *our time*. We can give each other feedback. And check out, y'know, if we've got a future. This isn't a dress rehearsal, Laurence, this is the real thing. I wanna find the real me in this relationship. You wanna find the real you. We wanna find the real each other. Yeah?

Laurence   Yeah. But . . .

Gina   Are we agreed on that?

Laurence   Yeah.

Gina   Talk through y'feelings on that one, Loll, coz I need to know. Zero talk means zero communication, yeah?

Laurence   Yeah.

Gina   So talk.

Laurence   Erm. I think. We've gotta . . . listen to each other. And . . . hear each other.

Gina   And listen to your heart?

Laurence   Oh, God, yeah.

Gina   Like your inner voice?

Laurence   Like the inner child.

Gina (*nodding*)   With yeh, with yeh.

Laurence   Coz like . . . zero contact . . . means zero everything, really.

Gina   When you say contact . . . d'you mean like on a spiritual level?

Laurence   Well, spiritual and . . .

Gina   Psychological?

Laurence   Yeah. And, y'know, I think . . . sometimes . . . words aren't enough.

Gina   That's why classical music's so popular with old people.

Laurence   Exactly.

Gina   Right, so can I do a recap here? What you're saying is . . . sometimes, verbal communication doesn't reach far enough.

Laurence   That's exactly it.

Gina   Goway, so like, y'talking . . . psychic powers here?

Laurence   Well, that sort o'communication where, between a man and a woman, you can sort of reach out and . . . have a shag.

Pause. **Gina** *eventually stands up.*

Laurence   Tell me what y'feeling, love.

Gina   Caravan's this way you say?

She's walking away.

Laurence   I thought we were talking!

Gina   Give us that torch!

She snaps the torch out of his hands and storms off, fuming.

Laurence   Yeah, well, you said I'd get me hole in Tenby and look at yeh! I'm sick o'the sight o'you flirtin' with anything in a tracksuit. I've seen you with them lads from Kirkby in the third caravan down. You'll put a stop to that!

Gina   They're dead spiritual!

Laurence   I've seen yeh!

Gina   Drop dead!

Laurence   Gina! Wait for me! I said . . . ay, you!

He follows her off. Blackout.

Scene Two

The same, a few nights later. It is a bit lighter now, though still late at night. We can now make out a wire-mesh fence halfway down the stage. Lights flash past indicating a passing train on a railway line beyond the fence. **Liam** *comes on and walks slowly along. A* **Man** *enters in jogging gear. He half jogs and walks, then stays jogging on the spot.* **Liam** *freezes. The* **Man** *speaks with a broad Welsh accent and looks like he could be in the army.*

Man   Lost something?

Liam   Er, me dog.

Man   I haven't seen no dogs. Not from round here?

Liam   No.

Man   Holiday?

Liam   Yeah.

Man   Bring your dog on holiday, do you?

Liam   She's brown. 'Bout this high. Judy.

Man   Judy?

Liam   Yeah.

Man   It's not a good idea bringing dogs up here this time o'night. You wanna stick to the road.

Liam   I was on the road but I let her off the lead. She ran into the trees.

Man   Where's the lead now then?

Liam   Sorry?

Man   Dog lead.

Liam   In me pocket.

Man   Bit late for dog walking, init?

Liam   She needed a crap.

Man   I like the peace and quiet this time o'night. No cars on the road. No one to see you, jogging like. I can just run and run and . . . maybe she's gone down by the railway line. There's a hole in the fence. Maybe she's gone through there, had a bit of a sniff around and can't find the hole again.

Liam   D'you think so?

Man   It's easy enough to do. You've gotta know the fence, haven't you?

Liam   I hope she's all right.

Man   She won't be mown down by a train. There's another fence next to the line. Wire-mesh. No holes in that.

Liam   Perhaps I better look.

Man   It's only an idea. She could be anywhere, couldn't she?

Liam   Yeah.

Man   D'you want me to show you where the hole is?

Liam   Go 'ed then.

Man   I don't mind. It's better if you're with someone, don't you think?

Liam   Suppose so.

Man   It's down here.

He shows him the hole in the fence. They go through to the other side.

Liam   Can't see her, can you?

Man   What's your name, lad?

Liam   Wayne.

Man   Scouser?

Liam   How d'you guess?

Man   I used to know Liverpool.

Liam   Yeah?

Man   Staying up the caravans?

Liam   Yeah.

Man   With your mates?

Liam   Family.

Man   Still at school?

Liam   Just left.

Man   Which one?

Liam   Pope John Paul the Second.

Man   Good Catholic boy?

Liam   Dunno.

Man   Do much sport?

Liam   No. She's not here, is she?

Man   I don't think so.

Pause.

Ah, I need a slash you know.

Pause.

Think I'll have one. Don't mind, do you?

Liam   No.

*The **Man** turns his back on the audience. He walks up a bit.*

Man   Good thing about tracksuits, no flies to mess about with. You wanna get it out, you can. No problem.

Pause.

Here, look at this.

Liam *slowly approaches him.*

Man   Look.

Liam   Where?

Man   Is that a tenner down there?

Liam   It's just a bit of paper.

*A train goes past. They are momentarily lit up. **Liam** stares at the train in panic.*

Man   What d'you think of that?

Liam   It's all right.

Man   Yeah?

Liam   Yeah.

Man   Not bad, is it?

Liam   No.

Man   You shy, Wayne?

Liam   No.

Man   You sure?

Liam   Yeah.

Man   Well, go on then.

Liam   What?

Man   Let's see yours.

Liam   I've gotta find me dog.

Man   Fuck your dog.

Liam   Me mam'll kill me.

*The **Man** puts his dick away and turns round. He starts to walk away.*

Man   You had your chance, lad. No Scouser messes me around. Can't afford to be choosy with a face like that. Hanging round here. Bet you lose your dog every night.

Liam   She just ran off.

Man   Fucking Catholics.

Liam   Hang on!

Man   Why? What's keeping me here? You shouldn't play games with me I've told you.

Liam   I've never . . .

Man   Never what?

Liam   I mean I've watched. There's this field back home. I've seen. But. Never. I mean. I want to. But.

Man   But what?

Pause.

Eh?

Liam   Don't go.

Man   Why not?

Liam *undoes his trousers and pulls them down.*

Liam   Well, what are you waiting for?

Blackout.

Scene Three

A flat in London.

Joanne*'s flat in Earls Court. A big old room in a converted house. The only features are a sofa bed, opened out into a bed, and a window.* **Joanne** *is a woman* **Terry** *has met in the pub that night.* **Terry** *comes in and stares at the bed. He sits on it.*

Terry   Nice flat.

Joanne *comes in with two drinks. She's a good-looking thirty-year-old with a north London accent. She hands him a drink.*

Terry   Couldn't you afford a couch?

Joanne   Oh, sorry, it folds away into a settee. I weren't expecting to bring anyone back. Come on, give us an hand.

She goes to put the bed back into a settee. **Terry** *stays sitting there.*

Terry   No, it's fine.

Joanne   Right. It's vodka and orange, it's all I had in.

Terry   So what do they call this then?

Joanne   According to the letting agency it's a spacious pied-à-terre for a single person or couple in the heart of cosmopolitan Earls Court. But as far as I'm concerned it's a room in a house on the fourth floor with no lift. And as for Earls Court being cosmopolitan, that means that every other person you meet is a queen, a brass, a backpacker, or a nut-nut.

Terry   And what are you?

Joanne   Pissed. Hopefully. The amount you've spent on me tonight.

Terry   But how would you describe yourself?

Joanne   To who?

Terry   In that little list.

Joanne   Well, I aint a queen.

Terry   Are yer a brass?

Joanne   You know exactly what I am, Terry.

Terry   Why d'you think I come back?

Joanne   Why? Well, the way I remember it was, we was having a laugh in the pub with your mate Charlie and us two wanted to keep on drinking.

Terry   He's all right, Charlie.

Joanne   Suppose.

Terry   No he is.

Joanne   Yeah, well, you aint seeing it from my perspective. As soon as a bloke finds out what I do for a living he just can't let it drop. 'You're beautiful! You're too intelligent.' Load of old wank. Whereas you. You spoke to me like I was a human being.

Terry   Fuck, are yeh?

Joanne *smiles.*

Joanne   Come on. Let's make the bed into a couch. I can't get comfy.

Terry   I'm all right.

Joanne   Oh, well, that's all right then.

Terry   Have I missed the last tube?

Joanne   No. Why, d'you want to?

Terry   I like you, Joanne.

Joanne   But?

Terry   I haven't been honest with you.

Joanne   I know you're married.

Terry   No, it's not that.

Joanne   If you miss the last tube there's a cab office downstairs. There's buses all through the night. You're not in Liverpool now.

Terry   You can say that again.

Joanne   I'm not making you stay. (**Terry** *has finished his drink.*) My my, we were thirsty. Care for another?

Terry   Go 'ed then.

Joanne   I love your accent.

Terry   I haven't got an accent. I talk proper me.

Joanne   Yeah, yeah.

Joanne *exits.* **Terry** *gets up and goes and stands at the window. He puts his hand in his pocket and pulls his wallet out. He gets a bundle of money out of the wallet and goes and lays it on the bed. He puts his wallet back in his pocket and goes and stands at the window.* **Joanne** *comes back in with another drink. She hands it to him, then goes and sits on the bed.* **Terry** *remains standing looking out of the window, his back to her.*

Terry   Cheers.

Joanne   So what d'you make of London then?.

Terry   S'all right, yeah.

She finds the money on the bed.

Joanne   Terry, you've dropped …

Pause.

Terry?

Terry   I don't know how much you charge.

Pause.

I couldn't believe it when I first got here. Every phone box you went in just full of all these cards and numbers. Cards and numbers. Up for a good time? Dial this number. Yeah, I'm up for a good time. But I never had the bottle to dial. So I goes in another box and another box. And I just kept phoning our house. Which is pointless coz they're all away. So I just listen to it ring. And tonight. I goes in another box. Only this time I dial. Some fucking bird with big tits in Bow. I don't even know where Bow is. And she answers. And I hang up.

Joanne *is starting to cry, silently.*

Terry   I'm a shithouse, Joanne. I can't even get that fucking right. So I meets Charlie for a drink and you're there with your mates. And when you say what to do for a living, I'm like . . . Jesus. It's being handed to me on a plate. What am I gonna do? Only I can't even get this right. I'm looking at yer all evening like a moth to a flame. Only when a moth gets to a flame it's two steps forward and ten steps back.

Joanne   Look at me.

Terry   Only moths don't take steps, do they? They fly.

Joanne   Look at me!

Terry   I can't get nothing right!

Joanne   No you can't. Some punter you are if you can't even look at me.

He turns round.

See this? (*She holds the money up.*) I don't want this! I don't want jack shit from you!

She throws the money down on the floor.

Terry   Don't cry, babe.

Joanne   Don't you dare tell me what to do. Jesus, d'you think I brought you back here for . . . Make up your mind, Terry. What am I? An easy lay at the end o'the night? A mate? I'm certainly not Big Tits in Bow.

Terry   Please. Let me fuck yeh. I haven't fucked our Carol in six months.

Joanne   Good. And when was the last time you made love to her?

Terry   I'll make love to you then.

Joanne   D'you wanna know how I'd really describe myself? Stupid. I'm so stupid! I meet blokes like you all the time. You're just like all the rest.

Terry   I'm not.

Joanne   Well, what d'you call that then? You don't have to buy me, Terry. Why d'you have to go and spoil it?

Terry   I'm sorry.

Joanne   But I certainly aint giving it you for free now.

Terry   Can we start again?

Joanne   D'you know what makes me stupid? What makes me really stupid? I don't fancy many people. And tonight. Christ, why didn't I just say I worked in a shop?

Terry   D'you want me to go?

Joanne   Be a fucking man!

Pause.

Terry   What shop d'you work in?

Pause.

Joanne   Boots.

Pause.

Terry   Which counter?

Pause.

Joanne   Rimmel.

Terry   Worked there long?

Joanne   Since I left school.

Pause.

Terry   What's it like?

Joanne   I love it.

She's crying again now. **Terry** *takes her in his arms and kisses her.*
She responds.

Terry   I'm sorry.

Joanne   You're a good man, Terry.

Terry   I'm a waste o'fucking space.

Joanne   Bet Carol don't think so.

Terry   You're beautiful.

Joanne   Don't.

They kiss again and fall on to the bed. It looks like they're going to have
sex. **Joanne** *undoes* **Terry***'s belt and starts pulling his jeans down.*
He panics and tries to pull away from her. She doesn't let him go
without a fight. He sits away from her.

Terry   Leave me alone. Leave me. Don't touch me.

Joanne   It's all right.

Terry   No it's not.

Joanne   You're just pissed.

Terry   I wish I was. I wish that was all it was.

Joanne   Let's just lie here.

Terry   I really do.

Joanne   Well, what is it? Drugs? I don't have that effect on too many people.

Terry (*laughs*)   You haven't got a fucking clue, have yeh?

Joanne   I've only just fucking met you!

Terry   I wouldn't worry. I've known our Carol most o'me fucking life and she doesn't know.

Joanne   What?

Terry   Me.

Joanne   I don't know what you want.

Joanne *tries to push him again. He brushes her off gently.*

Terry   What's that park called near Buckingham Palace?

Joanne   St James?

Terry   I was down there this avvy. And there was this duck there trotting along, with all its baby ducks following behind. Every turn it took the babies followed like a shadow. And he's heading for the lake. Only there's this fence. And he can't get through. He's too big. And he's looking for a gap, only he can't find one. And the babies just follow. And then the babies cotton on and they squeeze through. And he tries and he tries and he's just stuck there, watching the babies. And people are gathering round, tryina help it over. But he spreads his wings out and they can't get hold of him.

Joanne   And?

Terry   What?

Joanne   What happened then?

Terry   I couldn't look any more. That's me. The kids following. Then going on ahead. And you can't do nothing about it. And you're just stuck behind the fence and they're out there swimming. And people are tryina help you. But it's no fucking good.

Joanne   Sorry to disappoint you, Terry, but that duck was probably their mother.

Terry   And if that was our Carol she'da been all right. Let them go on ahead. Not panicking. I nearly lost me lads one day. But she doesn't understand. Coz she wasn't there. What's it gonna take for her to understand?

Joanne   I think you're asking the wrong person. Look. Why don't you stay? We don't have to have sex. Come on, it'll be really expensive in a cab.

He sits there. She takes his shirt off. She presses her glass to his chest to cool him.

Terry   OK.

Joanne   Nightcap?

He nods. **Joanne** *takes his glass and exits.* **Terry** *lies back on the bed. Something under a pillow is making it uncomfortable. He looks underneath it and finds a* Sun *newspaper. He is shocked. He jumps up and starts getting dressed again as* **Joanne** *returns with another drink for him.*

Joanne   What's up?

Terry   You read this crap?

Joanne   For the stocks and shares.

Terry   The lies they printed about Hillsborough.

Joanne   Oh shit.

Terry   D'you know what they said we did? They said we robbed dying kids of their money. Said we pissed on them.

Joanne   I'm sorry.

Terry   Have you ever seen anyone die?

Joanne   Me mum.

Terry   I bet you never robbed her.

Joanne   Terry . . .

Terry   Or pissed on her.

Joanne   Terry, stop it.

Terry   I seen so many people die that day. Right before me eyes. When a Scouser sees that he goes into shock. But Scouse shock doesn't mean you rob or piss on people. We're not an alien nation.

Joanne   I know.

Terry   Yet you still buy this filth?

Joanne   It was a long time ago.

Terry *gives a long pained laugh.*

Terry   And I've just got a scally working-class Liverpool chip.

He stands up.

Terry   Thanks for the drink.

Joanne   Don't I even get a kiss?

Terry   I'll see meself out.

He goes. **Joanne** *lies back on the bed as the lights fade.*

Scene Four

The beach at Tenby.

A few days later. **Marni** *sits in a deckchair on the pebbly beach. She has a summer dress on. There is another deckchair empty next to her.* **Carol** *walks towards her along the beach in a sarong and bikini top, carrying a big straw beach bag.*

Marni   Any sign?

Carol   They've gone out for a walk. I've done something terrible.

Marni   What?

Carol   I went in their caravan when they'd gone.

Marni   Oh, God. Call the police.

Carol   Well, it's a good job I didn't, coz I found this.

She opens her beach bag. **Marni** *pulls out a tin. She opens it and pulls out a joint.*

Marni   Where?

Carol   Is it what I think it is?

Marni   Where was it?

Carol   In our Laurence's toilet bag.

Marni   What were you looking in there for?

Carol   I wanted to see if he'd brought any johnnies.

Marni   And has he?

Carol   Thirty. Oh, what am I gonna say to him?

Marni   Slip it back later and he'll be none the wiser.

Carol   Is it pot?

Marni   One way to find out.

She lights it.

Carol   Marni! What are you doing?

Marni   I think it's skunk.

Carol   Oh, Marni, don't. It's a slippery slope.

Marni   Oh, goway! Queen Victoria used to smoke this stuff all the time.

Carol   Did she?

Marni   Didn't get her itching for a bit o'smack, did it?

Carol   What was wrong with her?

Marni   Nothing. She was always off her tits on this stuff.

Carol   Have you done it before?

Marni   Years back. When I was courting Col's mate Lenny McVitie from the Tate 'n' Lyle.

Carol   You never told me.

Marni   I never told you he tried to give me one up the arse but he did.

Carol   No, you did tell me that.

Marni   Did I?

Carol   You told everyone.

Marni   Will you relax, Carol?

Carol   Some kids out in a dinghy there, look.

Marni   I'll roll another one in a minute, then he won't know we've taken it.

Carol   We?

Pause.

Did you think it was tight of me not to give the kids money for a dinghy yesterday?

Marni   It's fucking good skunk this.

Carol   Just coz everyone else at the site was hiring them.

Marni   Paul McCartney smokes this stuff, you know.

Carol   I'm not made o'money.

Marni   Thirty johnnies? (*Giggles.*)

Carol   You don't think they're at it in the caravan, do you?

Marni   With your Liam front row in the audience? I don't think so.

Carol   I hope to God she's on the Pill. I should ask really. Me of all people.

Marni They probably nip down here to the beach of a night. I did that when I was their age. (*Lights the joint.*)

Carol I remember.

Marni You and Terry in one bed. Me and Charlie in the other. The babies in the carry cots. We were too embarrassed to even kiss in front of yous. I got bruises on me bum from all these pebbles. Charlie used to say, 'It's you, me and the stars, baby.' Like he was Jimmy Cagney or something. He'd lie on top o'me. And he'd just look down into me face like I was the most beautiful thing he'd ever laid eyes on. In awe of me.

Carol Ah.

Marni Now we can't have so much as a light on. If there's a chink in the curtains he has to get up and mess about wit them. Can't bear to look at me.

Carol Marni.

Marni It's true. He doesn't even kiss me any more. Just sticks it in. When he can find it. And gets on with it. I'm like that: 'Pull me nightie down when you've finished.'

Pause.

Carol It's hard when you have kids though. Keeping the noise down. Sorry.

Marni No. I was just thinking. If someone had come to us, when we first come here. When our Colin first found this caravan site. If someone had come to us and said, y'know, in twenty years' time . . . all this is gonna've happened to you. And shown us. I'd never've believed it.

Carol No.

Marni And yet. All this has stayed the same. The caravan's still olive green.

Carol Vile.

Marni   The trees are still there. The sea's still there. Nobody's changed all this. Yet. Some bright spark with a clipboard hasn't gone, 'Ooh, y'know what'd go lovely there? A nice tower block.'

Carol *chuckles.*

Marni   But we've changed.

Carol   Have we? I still feel eighteen. I look at that Gina and wonder why I don't remember her from school. Get a fucking big shock when I look in the mirror.

Marni   I don't think I'll ever be the same again. All them miscarriages. Then Wayne. Wayne loved all this. I'm trying real hard, y'know. To be me normal bubbly self. Not to be mopy. I always knew that one day I'd sit on this beach, and look at that view, and not have him here. I always knew that one day we'd have an extra room gathering dust and not know what to do with his things. And I always knew realistically it'd be during his teens. I just suppose I thought that when I sat in this chair and looked at that view I'd have Charlie with me. Oh, I'm glad you're here. I want you here. I just thought he'd be here too.

Carol   Silly prick.

Marni   He was wrong, my Charlie. It's not me, him and the stars. It's just me.

Carol   Am I gonna get a drag on that or what?

Marni   Druggie. (*Passes the joint to her.*)

Carol   So? (*Takes a drag.*) D'you think those kids are all right over there?

Marni   Where?

Carol   They're miles away now.

Marni   They're probably local kids. Do it all the time.

Carol   God, it's heavy on your lungs, isn't it?

Marni   That's better.

Carol   Good. I can't remember the last time me and Terry even touched each other.

Marni   I can. A peck on the cheek when he said trar at the train station.

Carol   I feel like some old spinster. I should take up knitting.

Marni   Solitaire.

Carol   And yet. There was this time. We'd been married about a year. And he'd got his first car. You and Charlie babysat for us. And he drove us down to Otterspool Prom. And we made love in one o'them shelters on the front.

Marni (*shocked*)   It's dead open there!

Carol   I was shameless. I was in love. And we got back in the car. All blushes and giggles. And he put the radio on. And this song was playing. And he stuck the car in reverse and he drove me all the way down the Prom, backwards. And when we got to the end, the song finished. And he took my hand and kissed it and said, 'You'll always be my sex goddess.' And I knew he was full o'shite. And I knew we'd never do all that again. And I knew that moment had passed. But I didn't care. Coz we *had* done it. And we *had* driven backwards. And he *had* said it. Daft, isn't it? And I always thought he'd forgotten that. 'Til the week before Hillsborough. We went for a drive out on the Wirral. And we come across this sort of arts and crafts centre. And they had a record sale on, y'know, second-hand tapes and records. And I saw him buying this tape. And he sticks it in me handbag. And he whispers in me ear. 'Track four's for you, sex goddess.' And I looked at the back of the tape, and track four was . . . the John Lennon song 'Woman'. It's what had been on the radio that day. And . . . I felt so daft. Coz I thought only I'd remembered how special that day was. And I was wrong. It'd meant a lot to him too.

Marni   Stop hoggin' the joint.

Carol   I think you better roll another one.

Marni *chuckles. The lights fade.*

Scene Five

A dinghy in the sea.

Laurence, **Gina** *and* **Liam** *are in a dinghy in the middle of the sea. The lads are in trunks and T-shirts.* **Gina** *is in a swimming costume with a T-shirt over the top.* **Laurence** *is rowing with two oars, but having some difficulty.* **Gina** *is smoking.*

Gina   I can see yer ma over there, look.

Laurence   Don't let her see us.

Gina   Scared o'your own mother? Feel ashamed for yeh.

Liam   Is she looking?

Gina   Too busy gasbagging. With that mountain range she calls a friend.

Liam   Don't be vile, you.

Gina   Well, she does my swede in.

Liam   Oh, shut it, you.

Laurence   It's not her fault her son died, is it?

Gina   Not unless she sat on him.

Liam   Er, that's my best mate you're talking about there.

Gina   Well, you've gotto admit, she could do with losing a few pound. You're not peddling fast enough.

Laurence   It's rowing.

Gina   They're made up with the beach them two, they're never off it. K'nell.

Liam   You're made up wit the sound o'your own voice. You use it often enough.

Gina   Well, maybe that's because I know that one day, this country is gonna be listening to it, when I've got me own discussion programme. *The Gina Carmichael Show.* And I tell you one thing, *you'll* never be a guest on it. (*To* **Laurence**.) Yer ma's gettin' smaller, row faster. (*Tuts.*) Feel ashamed.

Liam   Why?

Gina   Eh?

Liam   Why d'you feel ashamed?

Gina   I just do, all right?

Liam   And what d'you feel ashamed of?

Gina   Oh, Laurence, will you tell him? He's doin' my swede in.

Liam   What d'you feel ashamed of?

Gina   You, if you must know.

Liam   You're in the middle o'the fucking sea. There isn't another person for miles. Who is there to feel ashamed in front of?

Gina   The fish. All right?

Liam   Ay, Laurence. Me ma's tiny now.

Gina   I've told him to row faster, he's just ignoring me. What's new?

Laurence   I'm rowing as fast as I can.

Gina   We must be miles away from the shore now coz that Marni one looks like a stick insect.

Liam   What y'doin', Lau'?

Laurence   It's dead hard.

Liam You'll never have yer own show.

Gina Wanna bet?

Liam Yeah, I do.

Gina Well, let's see the colour o'your money. See? You know I'm right. I met this DJ once from Radio City, and he said I had more than enough to . . . in his words . . . 'make it in this business.'

Liam The perfect face for radio. (*To* **Laurence**.) Let's have a go.

Gina Oh my God, where are we?

Laurence Oh, shut up, woman.

Gina But . . .

Laurence Shut up!

Liam We're drifting out.

Liam *is now having a go at rowing.*

Gina Y'know what this is, don't yeh? It's karma. I knew we shoulda paid for this dinghy.

Liam It wasn't my idea to rob it.

Pause.

You have a go.

Gina *takes over the oars.*

Gina I thought the beach was looking a bit quiet.

Laurence What are y'tryina say?

Gina The fucking tide's goin' out, isn't it? And us with it.

Laurence It was your idea to come out in this fucking dinghy.

Liam No wonder me ma said we couldn't.

Gina So it's my fault, is it? Ah, well, fuck y'fuckin' oars then!

She throws the oars into the middle of the boat. **Laurence** *picks them up and rows again.*

I'da tried anything to keep you out o'them woods. Y'dirty bastard. You've had one thing on your mind this holiday. It rhymes with kex, and when you do it, you don't wear 'em. Why d'you think I suggested Liam came an'all. To keep you off me!

Laurence We could swim back.

Liam You know I can't swim.

Laurence I could get in and try and pull the boat back as I'm swimming.

Gina A cunt y'maybe but I don't want you drowning on me, Laurence.

Liam What are we gonna do?

Gina HELP!!!

They all scream 'Help' for a while.

Gina It's so quiet.

Liam They say that just before a plane crashes it goes deadly silent.

Laurence What you sayin' that for?

Gina There isn't even any seagulls.

Liam I can still see me mum. MUM!!!!

They all call 'MUM!'

Laurence We're gonna be all right. She's seen us.

Gina What's she gonna do? Row out on her friend?

Laurence Just keep calm.

Liam She hasn't seen us.

Laurence   She has, look she's running down the beach.

Liam   Has she?

Gina   What if she's just goin' for an ice cream or something?

They call 'Mum' again.

Gina   What do we do now?

Laurence   Just wait. (*To* **Liam**.) Stop cryin', you.

Liam   I'm not.

Laurence   Y'big pufta.

Liam   Shut up, you.

Gina   He's scared.

Laurence   I'm fuckin' scared but I'm not cryin'!

Pause.

Gina   Scared o'dyin' a virgin?

Laurence   Scared o'dyin' a slut?

Liam   Will yous two stop it?

Laurence   Just coz you're gonna die a virgin.

Liam   We're not gonna die. Me mum's seen us.

Gina   Can't even see her now.

Liam   She'll get help.

Laurence   Little virgin fuckin' cryin'.

Liam   I'm not a virgin, all right?

Laurence   Oh and who've you fuckin' knobbed?

Liam   Mind your own.

Gina   I've heard stories about you.

Liam   I've heard stories about you.

Gina   Off my mate Yosemite who lives by the Backy. She's seen you hanging round with the queer boys of a night. On the mound.

Laurence   Well, she's fuckin' lying then.

Gina   Oh, you go sticking up for him, why don't yeh?

Laurence   She's speaking bollocks, he never even goes out hardly.

Pause.

Liam   Well, I've heard you. In the middle of the night. Stuffing your face. Then making y'self sick.

Pause.

Gina   I think there's something wrong with your hearing, love.

Liam   Don't love me.

Gina   Don't worry, Liam. I'll never love you.

Pause. She sings.
    In my Liverpool home
    In my Liverpool home
    We speak with an accent exceedingly rare
    Meet under a statue exceedingly bare.
    If you want a cathedral, we've got one to spare
    In my Liverpool home.

Laurence   What d'you sing that for?

Liam   Me ma's gonna kill us.

Laurence   I know.

Pause.

Gina (*sings*)
    In my Liverpool home
    In my Liverpool home
    We speak with an accent

Liam (*joining in*)
    exceedingly rare
    Meet under a statue exceedingly bare
    If you want a cathedral, we've got one to spare.

Laurence (*joining in*)
    In my Liverpool home.

They start to sing it again. The sound of a helicopter arrives overhead. It starts to drown them out. They look above them and stop singing, happier now. As the lights fade a rope ladder descends towards them from above.

Scene Six

The caravan site.

That evening. The two deckchairs now outside the caravans. **Carol** *sits smoking a joint in one of the chairs looking at a Welsh paper.* **Marni** *enters with a bag of shopping. There's a picnic table housing beakers and food.*

Marni   Carol! What are you doing?

Carol   Did you get any Silk Cut? I had to roll this with one o'your Consulate, it's vile.

Marni   I can smell that from here. What if the kids come out?

Carol   They'll think I'm Queen Victoria.

Marni   You're terrible, you are.

Carol   It's only a little one. I put the rest of it back in his bag when he wasn't looking.

Marni   Pass us them beakers.

Carol *passes her some beakers off the table.* **Marni** *pours two brandies.*

Carol   Was the shop open?

Marni   No, I nicked a car and ram-raided the offy. Get this down your screech.

Carol   I can't believe it's in the paper.

Marni   I can't believe it's in Welsh. They coulda written all sorts about yeh and y'wouldn't know.

Carol (*looking at picture in paper*)   Typical Gina. She's just been dragged out the sea by an 'elicopter and she sticks her full slap on for the camera. Look at the smile on her. She looks like Samantha Fox.

Marni   Did she get through to her mother?

Carol   Yeah. Right after I spoke to Terry. What's she gonna think of me lettin' 'em go out in a dinghy?

Marni   You didn't.

Carol (*knocks back her drink*)   That's better.

Marni   Are they in the caravan?

Carol   Gina's gone the phone. Wants to see if there's any trains tonight.

Marni   You can't blame her.

Carol   I wish Terry was here.

Marni   I know. I know Charlie can be a soft cunt an' all that, but this week's been the one time I've actually missed smelling his lager breath last thing at night. I've even missed stickin' me earplugs in coz of his snoring. Getting a waft of his sweaty farts when I move the duvet.

Carol   We should've made them come with us.

Marni   We'll be all right.

Carol   God, Marni, I feel really weird. I mean, I'm dead happy and relieved . . .

Marni   You're in shock.

Carol   D'you want some of this?

Marni   Quick drag.

Carol   What are we like? All these other people must think we're fuckin' headcases. Smoking pot. Goin' out in dinghies when the tide's goin' out. Air-sea rescues. Hardly giving Liverpool a good name, are we?

Marni   Half these people are from Liverpool, y'melt.

Carol   Oh, here's Gina.

Marni *stubs out the joint.*

Carol   Hiya, love! Y'oright?

Gina *enters.*

Gina   Yeah.

Carol   Is there a train?

Gina   That family from Kirkby are going home tonight and said they'd give us a lift.

Carol   Are you sure?

Gina   I didn't imagine it.

Carol   No, are you sure you wanna go with them?

Gina   Yeah. I can get a bus straight back to Halewood from theirs.

Marni   Fair enough.

Gina   I better tell Laurence.

She exits.

Carol   He'll be fuming.

Marni   I know. I think he's a bit jealous of her even talking to them lads, never mind accepting lifts off them.

Carol   You don't think the kids are bored, do yeh?

Marni   Carol. Lighten up.

Carol   Oh, Marni, you must think I'm so selfish.

Marni   Life goes on, girl. And if Wayne was still here you can bet your bottom dollar he'da been in that boat. Getting up to mischief. I'da given him a piece o'my mind. And then a big hug. And a soppy wet kiss. Then I'da given him a tenner and sent *him* down the shop for brandy and fags. Lazy hole here.

Pause.

But then he'd've been back, coz they wouldna serve him coz he was too young. So I'd've had to go.

Pause.

Gets me through the day.

Carol   He mighta got served. He looked older than fifteen.

Marni   I shouldna sent him in the first place.

Carol   You coulda gone together.

Marni   Yeah. He was a good boy like that. I used to go in that garden for a ciggie and I'd think positive. I'd think it was good that he'd never smoke, on account of his lungs. But now I think, God, what sort of a life is that? When you can't do anything wrong, can't nip out for a sly fag when your mother's back's turned. All your body'll let you be is good.

Carol   He had his music.

Marni   I'm still paying off his violin. When he played that solo at the school concert I coulda burst wit pride. I still could. Why haven't I broken down yet, Carol?

Carol   You will.

Marni   What if I don't?

Carol   You will.

Marni   If I didn't know meself better I'd say I was one hard-faced bitch. Ay up, there's a taxi coming. Wonder if it's for that family from Kirkby?

Carol   No, there's someone in it.

Pause. They stare off.

Oh my God.

Pause. Eventually **Terry** *enters with suitcase and a plant in a pot.*

Laurence? Liam?

Terry   I had to come, Carol. You didn't mind, did yeh?

Carol   Mind? You soft prick I'm made up!

They hug.

Laurence? Liam?

Terry   I jumped on the first train. Hiya, Marn.

Marni   Oh, she was just saying.

Carol   They're watching telly. Come on in.

Marni   How's Charlie?

Terry   He sends his love.

Carol   What's that?

Terry   I wanted to get you flowers at the station but they only had plants.

Carol   Stick it there. Hey! Square Eyes! Look who's here!

They exit. **Marni** *sits there. The lights fade.*

Scene Seven

The Fitzgibbons' lounge.

A week later. **Carol**, **Laurence** *and* **Terry** *sitting snugly on the couch watching the television.* **Laurence** *is in the middle.*

Carol   Not seeing Gina tonight?

Laurence   No.

Carol   Seeing her tomorrow?

Laurence   At work.

Carol   What about in the evening?

Laurence   I've got a driving lesson.

Terry   I suppose we should be grateful we don't have to listen to her wittering on about Ricki bloody Lake.

Carol   Oh, you should've heard her at the caravan, Terry. Every day we got a detailed description of what Ricki eats for breakfast, what Ricki eats for tea, or rather what she doesn't eat.

Laurence   I don't think she'll be happy 'til she's licked Ricki Lake out.

Carol   Don't be disgusting! Oh, that's horrible!

Laurence *and* **Terry** *are laughing.*

Terry   You dirty bastard!

Carol   Don't encourage him, you! You're as bad as each other! Eugh! God, I've got a really vivid picture in me head now.

Laurence (*about a woman on telly*)   She's a dyke.

Carol   Who?

Laurence   Her.

Terry   No she's not. Is she?

Carol   Is she, Lau'?

Laurence   Yeah.

Carol   No she's not. She's married to thingy. Him off what d'you call it. Shite thing wit vets.

Laurence   Nah, it just looks like her.

Carol   God, I wish you hadn't said that about Ricki Lake. Is she lesbian?

Laurence   Dunno. Probably.

The doorbell rings twice.

Carol   That's Marni's ring.

Laurence   She's another one.

Carol   You can answer the door for that.

She laughs as he leaves the room.

He's got a filthy mind on him. Aren't you shocked?

Terry (*not convincing*)   Yeah.

Carol   Yeah, thought you might be.

Terry   He's got a fucking brilliant sense of humour, our Laurence.

Marni *and* **Laurence** *re-enter.* **Laurence** *slumps back on the sofa,* **Marni** *sits in an armchair.*

Carol   Hiya, Marni love. (*To* **Laurence**.) Switch that off.

Laurence   I'm watching it.

Carol   Well, turn it down then. Ah are yer all excited, love? Got your Charlie coming home from the Big Smoke. Ah, are y'cooking him a nice tea?

Marni   No.

Carol   Are yous getting a Chinese? Spend his money.

Marni   I'm a cooking a nice tea, but he's not having any.

Carol   Why? What's happened?

Marni   Not unless I stick it in a Jiffy bag and post it to him in London. Waste o'good food.

Carol   Don't tell me! He's pissed in a bar and he's missed his train.

Marni   No.

Carol   Marni, what?

Marni   He's staying down there another week.

Carol   Goway!

Marni   Bastard.

Carol   Why?

Marni   They didn't get all the work done what with Terry coming back early so it's gonna take them longer. So he says.

Carol   Don't you believe him?

Marni   I wanna believe him.

Terry   It's possible.

Carol   Terry knows, y'know.

Marni   My brother is employing him as a favour. My brother would willingly pay him ten million quid and let him come home tonight.

Carol   Oh, have your tea with us.

Marni   No, I've got enough food to sink a battleship.

Carol   The money'll be good, love.

Marni   Who's side are you on?

Terry   She's not on anyone's side.

Carol   I'm on her side!

Laurence   Has he squared it with work up here?

Marni   Compassionate leave.

Carol   Maybe he wants some space. I don't mean from you.

Marni   Well, who from then?

Carol   From his head.

Marni   And what about me? I'm sick to death of space. I had a beach full of space in Tenby. I've got four walls and two floors of space through there. I need him here with me. That house has been empty for ages. Wayne only had about a week in his own bed the last six months. It's like nothing's changed. I get me coat on and me bus fare out and I get to the door and I look out to the bus stop and it's only then I remember. I can't go the hospital. I need Charlie here to make it real.

Carol   Oh fuckin'ell.

Marni   It's not too much to ask, is it?

Carol   No, it's not, Marni.

Terry   He's an arlarse, Marni.

Marni   Terry. I want you to be honest wit me now. Has he met someone else?

Carol   Don't be daft.

Marni   Has he?

Terry   No.

Marni   Swear on your Laurence's life.

Terry   I swear to yeh, Marni, no. I don't know what he's playin' at.

Carol   Marni, I'm quite sure.

Marni   I wouldn't blame him. I mean, look at me.

Carol   You're gorgeous, you.

Marni   I was once. Didn't realise it at the time. Now when I look at photos of meself when I was twenty I think, 'God, girl, you really had something.' Now I see a camera and I run a mile.

Carol   I'll kill that fuckin' Charlie. It's him that's made you feel like this. He doesn't know how lucky he is.

Marni   Well, I'm making lamb tonight if anyone fancies it. Roast potatoes, carrots, turnips, sprouts, mint sauce.

Carol   Oh, sounds gorgeous, count us in.

Marni   Diet starts tomorrow.

Carol   D'you fancy some o'that, Laurence?

Laurence   Yeah. You're a cracking cook, Marni.

Carol   And it better be dripping in fat or there'll be murders!

Marni   I'm so jealous o'you sometimes, y'know.

Carol   Oh, shut up.

Marni   I look at yous two and I'm green. You've got the kids. You've got each other. You've got a gorgeous figure, Carol.

Carol   D'you want a hand peeling the spuds?

Marni   And d'you know what the worst thing is? I know that in a week's time he's gonna ring up and say he's got to do another week.

Carol   Come on.

Marni   Will your Liam want to eat?

Carol   I suppose so. He's out walking Mrs R's dog.

Marni (*suddenly illuminating*)   I knew there was something I had to tell you!

Carol   What?

Marni Guess who I got speaking to in the Asda today?

Carol Who?

Marni Mrs Raymond. Can she talk for England or what? Well, you know you say your Liam's walking her dog right now?

Carol Yeah. He does it most nights.

Marni Well, I don't know whether he is actually.

Carol You what?

Marni I'm pushing some serious trolley round the Asda, getting all the bits in for arlarse's tea. When who should corner me in Home Bake but her.

Carol Mrs Raymond?

Marni I give her a quick nod, but you know how I've got one of those faces that people feel they can just gab at?

Carol Did you give her an inch and she took a mile?

Marni She goes, 'Scuse me, love, but don't you live next door to that nice Liam Fitzgibbon?' I goes, 'So?' coz, you know, I'm tryina get the tea in for *him*. She goes, 'Could you give him this?' (*Gets a tenner out of her pocket.*)

Carol Bloody'ell.

Laurence Bastard!

Marni I felt like saying, 'Give it him yourself, love. Who d'you think I am? The Royal Mail?' but then I caught sight of her zimmer frame and thought, anything to help an elderly neighbour . . . you know.

Carol Oh, isn't that lovely? Oh, he'll be made up with that.

Marni I haven't finished yet! Then she goes, 'I wanna thank him for making Judy's final days so special.'

Carol Judy the dog?

Marni Can you believe it?

Carol It's dead?

Marni Well, by this stage I'm thinking she's a bit barmy Miss Babs, so I goes, 'Let's get this straight, love. You're telling me that your dog is no longer with us?' She goes, 'Didn't Liam say? Run over on the bypass Tuesday last.' Then she bursts out crying. I had to leave me shopping where it was and help her to a cup o'tea in Beryl's Pantry. I got that fucking dog's life history. I felt like saying, 'Listen, love, I don't know what you see when you're twitching at your nets morning noon and night, but I happened to have buried me son two months back.'

Terry The dog can't be dead, he's walking it right now.

Marni Did you know the dog was blind?

Carol No.

Marni No. Neither did her from 34. She took the dog out while we were in Tenby, let it off the lead and, next thing you know . . .

Carol So where's our Liam been going?

Marni Spuds?

Carol Wait 'til I get my hands on him.

The phone goes. **Laurence** *answers it.*

I'll ring his bloody neck.

Laurence (*on phone*) Hello? Who is it? Hang on.

Carol Who is it?

Laurence *shrugs as he hands her the phone.*

Carol Hello? Speaking. Which station? I'll come and collect him.

She puts the phone down.

Terry Who was that?

Carol   Police.

Terry   What?

Carol   Liam's been arrested.

Terry   Eh?

Marni   What for?

Laurence   Fuckin'ell.

Carol   They said they'd tell me when I got there.

Marni   Terry, drive her.

Carol   I'm all right.

Terry   I'll walk you.

Carol   I'll go on me own.

Terry   Sure?

Carol   You wait here. I'll phone you when I get there, let you know what's going on. Where's me bag?

Marni   No, Carol, someone should go with yeh.

Carol   Still jealous?

Marni   Come on.

The women exit.

Terry   What's all that about?

Laurence   Dad?

Blackout.

Scene Eight

The same, two hours later. **Laurence** *is looking out of the window.* **Terry** *is sitting staring into space in the armchair. The telly is on.* **Laurence** *suddenly hurries back to the couch. The front door goes.* **Liam** *comes in.* **Carol** *follows with a brolly, putting it down.*

Liam *sits on the couch.* **Marni** *follows on behind. They all stay there in silence.* **Laurence** *breaks it.*

Laurence   You all right?

Liam *shrugs.*

Marni   Listen, I'll get the tea on.

Carol   No, stay, Marni.

Carol *is annoyed that* **Terry** *hasn't said anything. She switches the telly off, stands behind his chair and pushes it round so that he has to look at* **Liam**.

Terry   What did they say?

Laurence   Are they going to prosecute?

Pause.

Liam   Got let off with a caution.

Pause.

Terry   Well, that's good, isn't it?

Marni   That's what I said.

Terry   He's not been right since Hillsborough.

Laurence   This has got nothing to do with Hillsborough, Dad!

Marni   Look, I should go.

Terry   That put yer off y'footy.

Laurence   It's got fuck all to do with that!

Carol   Don't you swear at your father.

Liam   It's to do wit me.

Carol   Oh, so yer enjoy it, do yeh?

Pause.

Marni   I'll give yer a knock later.

Terry   Yeah, always sticking your fucking oar in.

Carol   Ay, you! She's more use to me than you are!

Liam   I never enjoyed footy.

Terry   Yes you did.

Marni   I'm not standing for this.

Liam   Stay, Marni!

Terry   You used to love football!

Liam   I never!

Terry   Yes you did! I used to take you up that Backy and have a kickabout and you loved it!

Liam   I just enjoyed spending time with you! I didn't care what I was doing!

Terry   Your face in the car down to Sheffield.

Laurence   For Christ's sake, our Liam's being doing it with fellas up the back field of a night. That's what this is about! Not football.

Carol   It's about him lying through his back teeth about walking some arl woman's dog.

Marni   Dead dog.

Liam   You know then.

Terry   Why did you do it, son?

Carol   At last!

Terry   Why did you do it?

Liam   Dunno.

Terry   Eh?

Laurence   Coz he enjoyed it probably.

Carol   Stop tryina help him out, you.

Liam What's so wrong with that?

Carol You're sixteen years of age! That's what's wrong with that!

Laurence You fucking hypocrite!

Terry Ay! Less of the swearing!

Laurence Well, you were pregnant with me when you were his age!

Marni That was an accident!

Liam So he was an accident, was he?

Terry No!

Laurence Well, thanks a fucking bunch!

Carol We weren't flying in the face of nature.

Marni Yeah, your mother certainly didn't go traipsing round the Backy having it off with lezzies, did she?

Laurence I dunno, do I?

Carol You cheeky bastard!

Marni You're a bright lad!

Laurence D'you have to be thick to be queer?

Terry He's not fucking queer!

Liam Aren't I?

Pause.

Marni Jesus Joseph and Mary.

Carol (*to* **Terry**) This is your fault, coz you weren't strong enough as a father.

Marni Yeah!

Terry Ay, what's it got to do with you?

Carol Stop having a go at her!

Terry   Take a look in your own backyard first!

Marni   Meaning what?

Pause.

Meaning what?

Liam   No one did this to me.

Laurence   There's nothing wrong with him. You gotta stop using Hillsborough as an excuse.

Terry   I don't.

Carol   At least he's got an excuse.

Liam   He hasn't though.

Laurence   He doesn't need an excuse!

Liam   We're both alive.

Marni (*to* **Terry**)   You fucking bastard!

Terry   Well, your Charlie spotted it years back!

Liam   You thought you'd lost us.

Marni   He never! He woulda told me!

Terry   I'm not surprised he hasn't come back!

Liam   You thought you'd lost us but yer hadn't.

Marni   Our Wayne was the nicest lad on this planet!

Carol   What are you gonna do, Terry?

Liam   We never died!

Terry (*to* **Carol**)   D'you want me to go mad? Kick him out? What is it you want, Carol?

Carol   Oh, since when has it mattered what I want?

Liam (*a roar*)   Will somebody just fucking listen to me?!

They all go quiet.

Liam   Please.

Carol   Well, say something then.

Marni *has broken down crying.*

Terry   I heard him. Yous all think I just sit here in me own little world. But I hear you. All of yous.

Laurence (*pointing out* **Marni**'s *distress*)   Mum.

Terry   You've hit the nail on the head, Li'. I thought I'd lost yous and I hadn't. And I vowed to meself that day that I wasn't gonna fucking lose yous if I could help it. So I won't be kicking no one out.

Carol   I'm not saying kick him out.

Liam   I'm sorry.

Laurence   Don't fucking apologise, Li'.

Terry   But I'll be fucked if you think you're going that Backy again.

Carol   Hallelujah!

Liam   You can't stop me.

Terry   D'you wanna bet?

Marni   Liam, you can't.

Liam   I bet Wayne would.

Carol   Liam, I think you better get to bed.

Liam   Oh, I'm sick o'living in this house.

Terry   Eh?

Carol   You what?

Laurence   You're not the only one, mate.

Liam   Living under your roof and his cloud.

Carol   I think it's your bedtime actually, Liam.

Liam   April comes and he's depressed.

Carol   Get to bed.

Liam   Can't bear the truth in this house. That's why you're always getting me to shut up.

Liam *goes to leave the room.*

Terry   Come back, you. Got something to say, Liam? Then say it.

Liam   You feel guilty.

Terry   Eh?

Liam   You blame the police. You blame the *Sun*. You blame everyone but yourself.

Terry   So Hillsborough was my fault, was it?

Liam   No!

Laurence   Let him finish. Jesus.

Liam   And . . . not getting over it. It's like you are blaming yourself.

Carol   Oh, I've had enough of this.

Laurence   That's precisely what he's saying, Mum. Open your gob in this house and someone has to jump down it.

Liam   And that's what they want. The police. The *Sun*. You slag them off to anyone who'll listen, Dad, and I know why.

Terry   Coz they're fucking bastards, the lot of them.

Liam   No. Coz you've let them get to you. Coz you were scared.

Terry   So?

Liam   And you tried to get out that cage. And when you did you stood on a kid. And you feel you killed him.

Pause.

Terry   I did.

Liam   Dad, you never. I never. He never. They did.

Terry   I did.

Marni   No you never, Terry.

Terry   Will you fucking shut it?

Pause.

Liam   And you think me ma doesn't understand coz she wasn't there. Well, where were you in Tenby, Dad? You'da seen she understood then.

Terry   I came as soon as I could!

Carol   Don't bring that up.

Laurence   Why not?

Carol   Just don't!

Laurence   Why not?

Liam   I thought you were going to kill us in Tenby, Mum. But you never.

Carol   Drop it!!

Terry   Carol?

Carol   Just drop it, Terry.

Marni   D'you wanna ciggie, Carol?

Carol   Do I? Do I? What do I want? I dunno what I want any more. I don't want this. But I've got it. I don't want to feel like me heart's about to explode but I've got it. I don't want you thinking I don't know me arse from me elbow but I've got it.

Terry   I don't think that!

Carol   And d'you know something else, son? You're right. I do know how your father feels, and d'you know what? It's sick. It's scary. And it frightens the living daylights out of me. All I ever wanted was a nice home, good kids, and enough money to see us through. Not much to ask, is it? I can't even manage that. Coz every now and again something comes along and smacks me round the face. I don't know what it is. But it says: You stupid cow. How dare you want that? I'm gonna take your kids away from you. Your nice home. That fella who said he loved you. I'm gonna take that all away from you coz you're a stupid bitch to want it in the first place.

Pause.

Marni   I want Wayne.

Liam   I'm sorry. About tonight. The Backy. I'm sorry.

Carol   Bed.

Liam *exits.*

Marni   I want Wayne!

She runs from the room.

Carol   Yous two are thick as thieves all of a sudden.

Laurence   Ah, I'm going to bed.

Carol   What for? So you can take some drugs?

Laurence   I'm surprised I'm not a smackhead having you as a mother.

Laurence *exits.* **Carol** *runs to the door.*

Carol   You cheeky little bastard! (*To* **Terry**.) Are you just gonna sit there and let him talk to me like that?

Pause.

Well, are yeh?

Suddenly **Terry** *jumps up out of his seat, he rushes to the door.*

Terry   Ay, you! Get back in here. I said get back in here! And you an' all, Liam!

Laurence *re-enters, closely followed by* **Liam**.

Terry   Got something to say to your mother, Laurence?

Laurence   She's the one who was kickin' off.

Terry   Have you got something to say to your mother,
Laurence?

Laurence   But . . .

Terry *smacks* **Laurence** *round the face. It stuns him. Pause.*

Laurence   I'm sorry.

Terry   Open your fuckin' mouth!

Laurence   I'm sorry.

Terry   Say it like you fucking mean it!

Laurence (*yells*)   I'm fuckin' sorry!! All right?!

Terry   Up them stairs.

Laurence *exits.* **Liam** *is cowering.*

Terry   And you? D'you know how it feels to get a phone
call from the police? Oh no, didn't think about that before
you went off gallivanting, did yeh?

Liam   I've said I'm sorry. I am. And I'm sorry I said that
about Wayne to Marni. But it's the truth. Wayne was me
best mate. I knew him better than any of yous.

Terry   OK OK, your mother's been through enough for
one night. But bear in mind you're grounded.

Liam   How long for?

Terry   Till I say. Now up them stairs. And if I were you
I'd be saying your prayers.

Liam   Marni's locked herself in the bog.

Liam *exits.* **Carol** *sits down.*

Terry   Give us one o'them.

She gives him a cigarette. He lights it up and they both sit there a while, smoking.

Carol   I better get up there and get her out.

Terry   Give her five minutes.

Pause.

Carol   What?

Terry   Is that how you feel?

Pause.

When was the last time that car was used?

Carol   I dunno. Monday? Frankie from the Heights took Laurence out for a lesson.

Terry   So there's petrol in it?

Carol   I dunno. I suppose so. Why?

Terry   Streets'll be quiet this time o'night.

Carol   Don't tell me you're gonna get behind the wheel o'that car. You'll be too scared o'knockin' some insomniac toddler over.

Terry   Come here, you.

Carol   Why should I?

Terry   Coz I'm yer husband and I say so.

Carol   It doesn't suit you, Terry.

Terry   Carol. For once in my life I'm fucking trying!

She gets up and goes over to him.

Closer.

She steps closer. He pulls her to him. He snogs the face off her. His hands are all over her.

Carol   Bloody'ell.

Terry   Get your coat.

Carol (*she still has it on*)   Are you blind?

Terry   The crap'll still be here when we get back.

He goes to the sideboard. He gets a tape out. He throws it to her.

Catch!

Carol   What's this?

Terry   Sounds.

Carol   John Lennon?

Terry   Where are the keys?

Carol   On the hook in the hall. Where they always are.

Terry   Come 'ed then.

Carol   Where are you takin' me?

Terry   Where d'you think?

He holds the door open for her and she goes out. He follows. Presently we hear the front door go. **Laurence** *comes down from upstairs and runs into the lounge and looks out of the window. Off, we hear* **Terry** *trying to start up the car.*

Laurence   Liam! Liam! Look out the window!

Outside, the car won't start.

Liam! Liam! Are yer awake?

Liam *appears in the doorway. He's got a coat on and he's packed a sports bag.* **Laurence** *is quite shocked.*

Laurence   Have you seen this?

Liam *stays where he is. Outside, we hear the car start up and then drive off.* **Laurence** *looks back.*

Laurence   Where are yeh goin'?

Liam   Never you mind.

Laurence D'you need some money?

Liam Please.

Laurence Tenner do yeh?

Liam *nods.* **Laurence** *gets a tenner out of his pocket and gives it to him.*

Laurence It's mad, isn't it?

Liam I know. Tar.

Laurence Well, if you're going, go. Marni'll be back down in a minute.

Liam Why you being so nice to me?

Laurence If I was being nice I'da give yeh twenty.

Liam *goes to the door.*

Laurence Are yeh goin' off wit one o'them fellas?

Liam Dunno yet.

Laurence Was you and Wayne?

Liam No.

Laurence I don't know nothing about this, all right?

Liam Yeah. See you, Laurence.

Laurence See you, Li'.

Liam Thanks. For the money.

Laurence *looks out of the window.* **Liam** *exits. The front door goes.* **Laurence** *watches* **Liam** *walk down the street. He gets a cigarette out and lights up. As he smokes, 'Woman' by John Lennon starts to play and the lights begin to fade.* **Laurence** *is keeping watch at the window, occasionally dragging on the cigarette.*

A SELECTED LIST OF
METHUEN MODERN PLAYS

☐ CLOSER	Patrick Marber	£6.99
☐ THE BEAUTY QUEEN OF LEENANE	Martin McDonagh	£6.99
☐ A SKULL IN CONNEMARA	Martin McDonagh	£6.99
☐ THE LONESOME WEST	Martin McDonagh	£6.99
☐ THE CRIPPLE OF INISHMAAN	Martin McDonagh	£6.99
☐ THE STEWARD OF CHRISTENDOM	Sebastian Barry	£6.99
☐ SHOPPING AND F***ING	Mark Ravenhill	£6.99
☐ FAUST (FAUST IS DEAD)	Mark Ravenhill	£5.99
☐ POLYGRAPH	Robert Lepage and Marie Brassard	£6.99
☐ BEAUTIFUL THING	Jonathan Harvey	£6.99
☐ MEMORY OF WATER & FIVE KINDS OF SILENCE	Shelagh Stephenson	£7.99
☐ WISHBONES	Lucinda Coxon	£6.99
☐ BONDAGERS & THE STRAW CHAIR	Sue Glover	£9.99
☐ SOME VOICES & PALE HORSE	Joe Penhall	£7.99
☐ KNIVES IN HENS	David Harrower	£6.99
☐ BOYS' LIFE & SEARCH AND DESTROY	Howard Korder	£8.99
☐ THE LIGHTS	Howard Korder	£6.99
☐ SERVING IT UP & A WEEK WITH TONY	David Eldridge	£8.99
☐ INSIDE TRADING	Malcolm Bradbury	£6.99
☐ MASTERCLASS	Terrence McNally	£5.99
☐ EUROPE & THE ARCHITECT	David Greig	£7.99
☐ BLUE MURDER	Peter Nichols	£6.99
☐ BLASTED & PHAEDRA'S LOVE	Sarah Kane	£7.99

• All Methuen Drama books are available through mail order or from your local bookshop.

Please send cheque/eurocheque/postal order (sterling only) Access, Visa, Mastercard, Diners Card, Switch or Amex.

☐☐☐☐☐☐☐☐☐☐☐☐☐☐☐

Expiry Date: _____ Signature: _____

Please allow 75 pence per book for post and packing U.K.
Overseas customers please allow £1.00 per copy for post and packing.

ALL ORDERS TO:

Methuen Books, Books by Post, TBS Limited, The Book Service, Colchester Road, Frating Green, Colchester, Essex CO7 7DW.

NAME: _____

ADDRESS: _____

_____

Please allow 28 days for delivery. Please tick box if you do not wish to receive any additional information ☐

Prices and availability subject to change without notice.

Methuen Contemporary Dramatists
include

Peter Barnes (three volumes)
Sebastian Barry
Edward Bond (six volumes)
Howard Brenton
  (two volumes)
Richard Cameron
Jim Cartwright
Caryl Churchill (two volumes)
Sarah Daniels (two volumes)
David Edgar (three volumes)
Dario Fo (two volumes)
Michael Frayn (two volumes)
Peter Handke
Jonathan Harvey
Declan Hughes
Terry Johnson
Bernard-Marie Koltès
Doug Lucie
David Mamet (three volumes)

Anthony Minghella
  (two volumes)
Tom Murphy (four volumes)
Phyllis Nagy
Peter Nichols (two volumes)
Philip Osment
Louise Page
Stephen Poliakoff
  (three volumes)
Christina Reid
Philip Ridley
Willy Russell
Ntozake Shange
Sam Shepard (two volumes)
David Storey (three volumes)
Sue Townsend
Michel Vinaver (two volumes)
Michael Wilcox